TRIKSTA

TRIKSTA

LIFE

AND

DEATH

AND

NEW ORLEANS RAP

Nik Cohn

Harvill *Secker*
LONDON

Published by Harvill Secker, 2005

2 4 6 8 10 9 7 5 3 1

First published in Great Britain in 2005 by
HARVILL SECKER
Random House, 20 Vauxhall Bridge Road
London SW1V 2SA

Random House Australia (Pty) Limited
20 Alfred Street, Milsons Point, Sydney,
New South Wales 2061, Australia

Random House New Zealand Limited
18 Poland Road, Glenfield,
Auckland 10, New Zealand

Random House South Africa (Pty) Limited
Isle of Houghton, Corner Boundary Road & Carse O'Gowrie,
Houghton, 2198, South Africa

The Random House Group Limited Reg. No. 954009
www.randomhouse.co.uk

A CIP catalogue record for this book is available from the British Library

ISBN 0 436 20535 1

Printed and bound in Great Britain by
Mackays of Chatham plc, Chatham, Kent

For Michaela, dime piece to the die.

CONTENTS

Some of the material in this book first appeared, in different form, in *Granta*, *The Guardian Weekend* magazine, and British *GQ*.

TRIKSTA

On a bright, chill January afternoon in 2000, I was strolling on Rampart Street, thinking of the pizza at Mama Rosa's, when a black male aged about ten walked up and spat at me, splattering my new Kenneth Cole leather jacket.

I have been obsessed with New Orleans for most of my life; it is the place I've loved best on earth. In recent years, however, it has turned violent and distressful, and getting spat on by a child, though mortifying, was hardly headline news. Another time, I'd have muttered a few choice curses and gone on my way. Only, this was not a good moment. I have hepatitis C, a virus that destroys the liver and feels, at least in my case, like permanent jet lag. For the most part, I've learned to handle it, but there are days when it handles me. The usual checks and balances cease to function, and I thrash about, untethered, driven by urges I don't understand and can't control.

This time I outdid myself. Instead of working out my spleen on some extra pepperoni at Mama Rosa's, I swung around and walked over to the Iberville project. Not a good idea. I had gone there the first day I ever spent in New Orleans, in 1972, and it had felt welcoming then, but the climate had changed. No outsider, white or black, with a lick of sense would choose to go strolling through the Iberville these days unless they had good reason. In my leather jacket, fat with credit cards, I was asking for trouble. Seeking it out, in fact.

Behind the abandoned hulk of Krauss's department store, I headed into the heart of the project. A few strides brought me to a blind corner. When I turned it, the sunlight was shut out. A few more strides, and a group of youths hemmed me in. None of them spoke or touched me, they simply blocked my path. The brackish smell of bodies was fierce, and I stumbled back against a wall as the youths moved in. Then, just as suddenly as they'd swarmed, they scattered. A city bus had turned the corner and fixed us with its headlamps.

I had never known worse fear. When I regained Basin Street and was safely in a taxi, I was surprised to find I hadn't pissed or shat myself. That was how it had felt back there—everything running out of me, uncontrollable. And what was most shameful of all, I knew my deepest dread had not been of getting robbed or even shot. I'd been afraid of blackness itself.

Afterward, I tried to blame it on the virus, or the light, or simple aversion to getting mugged. No dice. Over the years, I'd run foul of skinheads in London, neo-Nazis in Brooklyn, sundry policemen around the world. Though never brave, I had managed to keep up some vestige of front. In the Iberville, I was swept by blind animal terror, all pretense at dignity blown.

How could it be? Black music and black culture had been a huge part of my life; so had black friends and lovers. But those, depending on shifting fashion, were Negroes or African-Americans. They were nobody's *niggaz*.

The same friends and lovers had often told me this: all whites, cut them deep, are racist at core.

I remembered Kerry, a singer I dated some thirty years ago, and how one stoned morning, after we made love, she mocked my record collection, the posters on my walls, all the black artifacts I thought were part of me. Window dressing, she called them, and took my hand and placed it on her breast. This too, she said. She was in my bed, my world; that didn't mean shit. Drop me off in the ghetto, up against the wall, and see how I felt then. You'd turn cracker in a heartbeat, Kerry said. Of course, I refused to believe her. Other whites, maybe; not me. That poison couldn't be in me. Yet it was.

My home base is New York, but I visit New Orleans several times a year, often for months at a stretch. Usually, I rent a house, but this was a brief stopover and I was staying in Room 406 at the Villa Convento, a small pension on Ursulines Street, at the back of the French Quarter. My room, strewn with rap CDs that now seemed to mock me, faced onto the street. Deep into the night I lay awake, listening to the tourists trundling past on carriage rides and their guides pointing out the Villa as the site of the House of the Rising Sun, while I went back across my life, sifting through dirt—racial teasing that wasn't quite teasing, dumb drunken jokes, betrayals big and small. And what I saw in myself—bloated sack of half-truths and jive—was someone I couldn't live or die with.

I kept replaying those few seconds behind Krauss's, trying to pin down details. How many youths had there been? Could it be true that none of them spoke? And why in hell was I there, anyway? Who, finally, was I trying to confront? No answers came. All I could conjure up was a rush of amorphous bodies. Seemed like I'd been set upon by people with no faces.

At first light I rose and tried to scour myself in the shower, but the water wouldn't go past tepid, so I took a walk out of the Quarter through the Faubourg Marigny to the old black neighborhoods of Treme and St. Bernard, once thriving, now impoverished and falling down, heartachingly lovely still.

The streets were almost deserted—just a few homeless men scavenging or pushing shopping carts full of soda cans. At the corner of Pauger and Derbigny, a pickup truck swung by, two laborers on their way to work. A bounce song blasted on their radio; it sounded like 5th Ward Weebie. I felt the thump of bass in my bones and marrow, and a faint warmth seeped through me. The truck roared off along Pauger, raising yellow dust, and was gone in seconds, but the rumble of bass and Weebie's rap lingered. I started to walk behind them.

REGULAR JUGULAR

Soulja Slim was shot the night before Thanksgiving, 2003.

He was at his mother's house, the spacious duplex he'd bought her in Gentilly, out toward the lake, in a quiet neighborhood. Slim kept an apartment upstairs, which doubled as his studio.

The day of his death started well. The video for his new single, "Lov Me Lov Me Not," had arrived from New York. It was his come-back, his big shot at national stardom: "The start of the whole everything," his mother said later. After he'd got out of jail the last time, Slim had financed an album, *Years Later,* and put it out on his own label, Cut Throat Committy. It had sold more than thirty thousand copies in New Orleans alone, a phenomenal number for an independent release, and all the more so in this bootleg era, when maybe eighty percent of sales were off the books. Ten thousand was regarded as a hit these days; thirty was ghetto triple-platinum. Now Koch, a major label, had leased the album, added a couple more tracks, renamed it *Years Later . . . A Few Months After,* and was ready to give it serious promotion. At twenty-six, after thirteen years of rapping and over five years of jail, a heroin addiction and two near-fatal shootings, it looked as if Slim was finally on track.

In the afternoon some of his boyz from Cut Throat came by the house to watch the video. Everyone said it was hot. They planned to go in the studio and cut a new track later on, but first Slim had some errands to run. Around five he took off with his pardner

Trenity in his Escalade, customized with a flat-screen TV and the razor-slash Cut Throat logo carved into the seats.

By 5:45, when they returned, it was dark. Trenity got out of the passenger seat and went into the house, and Slim followed a few seconds behind. As a rule he stayed armed at all times, but this neighborhood was so peaceable, never a hint of trouble, that he let his guard down. His gun was still in the Escalade as he crossed the lawn and a man stepped to him out of hiding and shot him once in the back, three times in the face. Slim was dead before anyone could reach him.

I heard the news around seven. My phone rang, and a voice I didn't recognize started talking. Like most Southerners, rappers never bother to identify themselves. "Slim's gone," the caller said, then someone started yelling in the background and the line went dead.

A few minutes later, the phone rang again. And it kept ringing all evening. Some of the calls were from people I worked with and knew well, others from virtual strangers. These must have been working through their phone books from A to Z, speed-dialing at random. Though a few seemed surprised to hear a European voice, they plowed on regardless. Slim's death belonged to everyone.

Nobody seemed shocked. Slim had been running the streets, in harm's way, from a child, and he was famously confrontational. If anything, the wonder was he'd lasted so long. Even so, there was a sense of awe. A warrior had passed, a great man in his own world. Simply to help spread the news was a form of reflected glory.

It was three years since I had gone walking in the Iberville, two since I started working in rap, and killings had lost their novelty. Normally, when someone got shot, grieving was left to the family. For everyone else, it was more or less business as usual. At Wydell Spotsville's studio in Pigeon Town, a ravaged area near the Jefferson Parish line, I'd met a kid, fifteen at most. There was an eagerness in his face, a hunger that set him apart. I asked him to rap and he rattled off a verse, freestyling. One rhyme stood out among the standard gangsta posturing: "Need to maximize my worth / 'Fore I leave out this earth." I asked him to work on that thought and let me hear what came out, but he never showed up again. After a week or so, I asked where he was. "He got popped," someone said, and Wydell, a godly man, shook his head and sighed. Then he cued another track, and the kid was not mentioned again.

But Slim, that was different. A laundry list of local stars—Pimp Daddy, DJ Irv, Yella Boy, Kilo G, Warren Mays, and many others—had died by violence. Soulja Slim transcended them all. Though he'd never had a national hit, in New Orleans he was a giant. Only Juvenile and Mystikal were in the same league, and neither owned the streets like Slim. Now his legend was complete. Gunned down, he became an immortal—the city's Tupac, its Biggie Smalls.

In life, his talent had been instinctive and raw. He had the loose-lipped slack mouth, borderline speech impediment, that so many good rappers have, and a natural, low-slung flow, almost conversational. His verses were full of prophetic images, one foot in the Bible, the other in the gutter.

His greatest strength was authenticity. The raps were harsh, often vicious, but you knew instinctively that he'd lived every line of them. His was the voice of black New Orleans, in all its ugliness and beauty, its senseless slaughter, its moments of battered grace. He personified the split that lay at the city's heart—fierce joy in being alive, compulsive embrace of death.

At moments, he seemed to regret the lemming rush to self-destruct. On "Soulja 4 Life," he berated his generation and those who squeezed triggers with no hesitation for any little altercation. But a few weeks later, he was back to playing the outlaw, daring death: "I'ma still ride with my pistol though / An' drop the top on the low low so I can feel the wind blow . . ."

In another town, he might have worked through his conflicts

and emerged as an agent for change, but New Orleans didn't want that from him. No rapper had ever moved any records here by pushing messages. The only topics that sold were sex and killing, the more graphic the better. So sex and killing were what Slim served up, with a crazed abandon that none of his rivals could match.

Though we never met, we had many people in common. Among the musicians I worked with, Junie B had rhymed against him at porch contests when they were both coming up in the Magnolia, DJ Chicken and Shorty Brown Hustle had both known him well, Bass Heavy had produced some of his tracks. All, without exception, spoke warmly of him. He was strong medicine, you didn't mess with him. Rub him the wrong way, and he could be lethal. But he was generous and loyal, a straight shooter in every sense, and when he gave his love, it was absolute. In the rat nest of local rap, full of schemers and backstabbers, he lived by his own notion of honor, and nothing could shake him off it. "To me," said Junie B, "he was a decent person."

Myself, I loathed much of what he said but loved the way he said it. This night of his death, I sat listening to *The Streets Made Me,* his most cohesive album, and studied his face on the CD cover—thick-lipped and gold-toothed, with a blurry jailhouse tattoo of a crucifix between his eyes, a humorous twist to his mouth, and a wild spirit, at once ugly and beautiful.

Feeling claustrophobic, I moved outdoors to the porch. The house I was renting on Solomon Street, one block off Canal in Mid-City, had previously belonged to a Cajun couple, who'd lived there for thirty-some years, raised a family there, and had let the place crumble about them. It was a roomy stone structure, with plenty of space for the studio I'd set up in the back, but there was no heating, the electricity kept shorting, a 200-volt live wire dangled in one corner of the living room, deep cracks slashed the foundation pillars, and the front door was locked by a hook and eye that any toddler could have broken in. Never mind, I was contented here. My friend Nan had lent me her rocking chair, and the porch was set high above the street, on a level with a fine live oak. The orange glow of the crime lights came softly through the leaves.

Solomon Street was in transition. White gentry were moving in and buying up every house they could lay hands on. Nights, they sat gossiping on their stoops or walked their dogs on the sidewalks. The remaining blacks preferred to walk the center of the street, where they could see what was coming at them.

Tonight they moved in groups, talking about Slim's killing, and the mood was battlefront. Young bloods swaggered by in hooded jackets, sagging jeans. One of them caught me looking and cursed me out.

Around ten I got another phone call. Again I didn't recognize the voice, again the caller didn't bother to tell. After we'd waltzed for a space, he gave his name as Kevin and said we'd met the previous winter at the Warehouse, a now-defunct club, notorious for shootings, on Earhart Boulevard. I recalled that Little John's funeral parlor sat right next to the parking lot. Its slogan was "We mean business."

I'd scouted a couple of talent nights at the club and met a slew of rappers, and it was possible that Kevin had been among them. At any rate, he wanted to see me right away. He said he was in my neighborhood, then asked where I lived. "It's about Slim," he said.

I gave him my address.

Forty minutes passed, an hour. The phone had finally stopped ringing, and I was about to go to bed when a black Explorer pulled up, pumping Q93 on its radio: Lil Jon, "Throw It Up." The record was to the part where the East Side Boyz start yelling, "Back up bitch, get the fuck out my way." On this slumberous block, the thump, thump, thump of bass, mixed with Lil Jon's gravel roar, was a declaration of war.

As the driver's door opened, I saw a huddle of bodies inside, but only one got out. He came hooded up the steps, a long, lean shape with stooped shoulders, curved like a scimitar. When he stepped into the light and flipped back his hood, he was sporting an uptown fade, cropped hard to his skull. His features were African, blue-black.

It was a mobile, unsettled face, full of doubts. Though he had the hip-hop swagger and his mouth was full of gold teeth, he didn't look a hard case.

I didn't recognize him, though he seemed to know me well. "Mister Nik," he said, as if we'd parted minutes ago. He offered a plain white handshake, no tricky double-clutching or slithering palms. This was always a relief; I couldn't seem to master the choreography. No natural rhythm, I guess.

Kevin's touch felt clammy, and his eyeballs were red. He had been smoking too much of too strong; a tic jumped by his left eye. In the street below, his posse had rolled up the Explorer's windows and Lil Jon was dulled to a muffled thud. Even so, I could see or maybe just sense the suspension vibrating.

I offered Kevin a drink. "I'm straight," he said. Now that I had him in focus, I saw he was jittering. Maybe he balanced his smoke with speed, or he might simply be high-strung. Either way, his knee kept jiggling, and he didn't know where to put his hands. When I asked why he wanted to see me, he gave a start, as if he'd forgotten. "I was just passing through," he said.

We sat a few seconds in uneasy silence, then I mentioned Slim. The effect was like turning on a tape. "Something need to be done," Kevin said. This violence had to be cut out. It couldn't be that a man the magnitude of Slim got shot and it was like nothing, nobody took a lesson from it.

What did he suggest?

He wasn't sure. Maybe some kind of tribute record in the slain rapper's memory, with part of the profits going to a Stop the Violence fund. "Slim was my boy," Kevin said. "I woulda died for him, same way he died for me."

"Did you know him?"

"Everybody know Slim."

"Right. But *know* him."

"I was in jail with him." Kevin looked proud but defensive, as if I might call him a liar. "He was the truth, Slim. He stopped and talked with me many times, man to man. That's how he was, straight soulja through and through."

"What were you in for?"

"Transgression." His tic jumped and he ducked his head, avoiding eye contact. His hands lay spread on his skinny thighs, palms up. The fingers were long and slender, and so dark that the palms, by contrast, looked pink.

"Something need to be done," he said again.

I knew what he was getting at. He wanted me to put up some seed money, pay for studio time, and pitch the results in New York, where I was rumored to have friends in high places. In reality, my power contacts were minimal, but no one believed that down here. What would I be doing in the rap game, a white man heading for sixty, unless I had a hookup?

"I've never even heard you rap," I said.

"Give me a beat," said Kevin, "I'ma spit a verse right here."

I carried out the boom box from my living room and put on a sample track I'd scrounged from Don Juan. Kevin let a couple of beats go by, cleared his throat, once, twice, and started to freestyle the saga of Slim's life and legend, and how a bitch-ass nigga had killed his body but his spirit lived on, he was now Boss G in gangsta heaven.

The flow was ordinary, most of the rhymes third-hand, and Kevin kept losing his rhythm. I didn't care. Moments such as these make rap worth the freight. Recording is almost always hard slog. Twenty takes, the rapper's a wreck, the producer's wife is cheating on him, the engineer is too stoned to see the board, bit players keep butting in and giving bad advice, and the cell phones never rest. Hip-hop hell. But this—the porch above the street, the clinging damp of midnight, the crime light shining hazy through the live oak, the stuttering lurch of Don Juan's beat, the pink palms flashing and scything the thick air, the headlong rush of words, the sense of something being born—was rough magic.

By the time he finished, Kevin was sweating. All tension had drained away, and he was jubilant. "That's hype," he said.

Experience had taught me that what sounded good on the porch or in the living room usually turned into a pumpkin when committed to Pro Tools, the computer program on which much hip-hop (and other music) was recorded these days. Kevin's rap stood scant chance in the mass market and I'd be wasting our time to pretend otherwise. That didn't make it easy to tell him so. Given his chemical state, I half expected an explosion, but no, he just lowered his head and sighed.

Down below, the Explorer thudded and trembled, ready to be off, but Kevin was in no rush. Having made his pitch, he could relax and talk. "Conversation is an art," he told me. I must have looked surprised, because he laughed, a good laugh, soft and low. That was something his mother used to say, God bless her day. *Conversation is an art.* Also, *Time and tide wait for no man.*

He asked me where I came from, and this too was a surprise, for almost no one I'd met in rap had shown the slightest curiosity about who I was or what the rest of my life might consist of. I was just a man who'd fallen to earth; a man who might have a hookup.

"Europe," I said. "Northern Ireland. But New York is my home."

"You know Jay-Z?"

"I wish."

"I got a cousin lives in Brooklyn. Works in the subway, track maintenance. I'ma get up there and visit someday." His tic was hardly noticeable now; he seemed entirely at ease. "Ireland," he said. "You get much wildlife over there?"

"Such as?"

"Bears and tigers?"

Any chance he got, he told me, he watched the Discovery Channel. One day he hoped to visit Africa and live on a safari farm. "There's more to life than this rap shit," he said. "Rap's just a ticket out."

I'd heard similar remarks many times before. New Orleans was a backwater, locked in on itself. For most rappers here, the wide world was only a rumor. They might go to Houston on a dope run, or spend a few days in Atlanta for a glimpse of the fat life. When they had a record to promote, they performed in upstate Louisiana and the Florida panhandle, maybe Mississippi. A select few had visited New York or California, but the rest lived and rapped where they came from, and used the Discovery Channel as their magic carpet.

"They eat dogs in China," Kevin said. Deprived of smoke, he was slowing down. His eyes flickered, and it required a visible effort to rouse himself and slip back inside his hood. "I'ma holla at ya," he said in parting, and shook my hand again, another white handshake, goodbye. But goodbye isn't always gone. When he reached the street, another thought struck him, and he turned back. "You married, Mister Nik?" he said.

"Twenty years."

"How's it feel?"

"Feels good."

He stood a moment, considering this. "You're a happy man," he said at last, and opened the driver's door. David Banner's "Like a Pimp" blasted out.

*　　*　　*

Soulja Slim's mother, Linda Tapp Porter—Ms. Linda—is a ringer for her son. The same big bones and heavy features, the same wild but watchful eyes, and the same baleful stare when provoked. "A lot of Slim's friends, they can't look at me straight," she told me. "They say it's too much like looking at the dead."

It was a year after the murder before we met. For a long time, I didn't want to intrude. Then I read interviews with her in *Murder Dog* and other rap magazines, and again in the New Orleans *Times-Picayune*. Clearly, she was receiving. So I called her up one morning and went to see her that same afternoon.

She still lived in the same Gentilly house, a large stone building in a street so hushed and laundered it looked like a set for *American Beauty*. The spot where Slim fell was marked by a heart-shaped patch of flowers and a blonde, blue-eyed angel, presiding over a memorial stone that read *If Tears Could Build a Stairway, and Memories a Lane, I'd Walk Right up to Heaven and Bring You Home Again.*

The front room was a shrine, its walls covered with old album covers and other memorabilia—a painting that an inmate in Angola had sent, a pair of Slim's trademark black Reeboks, promotional flyers, glossies. The sense of his presence was inescapable. That was why Ms. Linda said she'd never move. "My son is here. If I leave, I'ma leave my son for real. I don't believe I could do that till I die outta this world."

She was a powerful woman, strong-minded and no-nonsense, and she spoke the rich tongue of New Orleans street speech, where children are *chirruns,* sneakers are *tennises,* loved is *loveded.* As A. J. Liebling once noted, it's an accent that has strong affinities to Brooklynese, both brogues handed down from nineteenth-century Irish laborers. So point becomes *pernt,* oil is *erl,* and if life isn't *dis,* it's *dat.*

We sat side by side on a sofa, facing a ragtag altar of Slim's effects. The feeling of quasi-religious observance was strengthened by the presence of Sandra, Ms. Linda's sister-in-law, here to bear witness and back up Ms. Linda's testifying, church-style, by echoing her words and occasionally moaning. "I knew God before Slim died, but not like I know Him now," Ms. Linda told me. "So many nights, after he was shot, I used to sit out on the porch and cry, waiting for someone to come and hold me, but it never did happen, no, till God came to me and told me I don't need nobody but God. That's when I joined Beacon Light. The preacher up there, he don't even know I'm Soulja Slim's mama; to him I'm just a soul in need."

She was doing better, she said. She still grieved, but she was to the place where she knew Slim wasn't coming back. And she took consolation from the fact that he was not forgotten. On the contrary, he was bigger in death than he had ever been alive. "Slow Motion," a song he'd sat on for years and finally shared with Juvenile, had come out last summer, six months after his killing, and gone to Number 1 on the *Billboard* singles chart, his first national hit. Now the same rappers who'd bypassed him while he was alive hailed Slim as a fallen hero. "My son is a legend," Ms. Linda said. "No one with a gun can take that from me."

Officially, the killing was still unsolved. A month after the murder, the N.O.P.D. had arrested one Garelle Smith, claiming he'd been paid ten thousand dollars for the hit, but they let him go for insufficient evidence. In any case, it wasn't the actual shooter that troubled Ms. Linda's heart. "I don't fault him," she said. He was on drugs and killed for drug money. The man behind him, the one who was too big a coward to face Slim himself, who hid behind his money and thought his life would be better with Slim gone, that was the one she had a problem with, her and God both.

"Jealousy killed him, that's my belief," she said. But what could she do? The police had let the shooter go, no great surprise. They'd always hated Slim in life, so why would they punish his killer?

They'd even found a snitch to claim that Slim himself had committed a murder for hire, shortly before his death; shot a man and cut him up and dumped the remains in the City Park lagoon, weighed down with cinder blocks. Anyone who knew her son would tell you that wasn't his style. "If you messed with him, I know in my heart you was asking for trouble." He didn't back down from anyone, but he was never sneaky, he did his business straight out. That snitch was flat-out lying, and the N.O.P.D. knew it. Slim wasn't here to defend himself, so they could say whatever. And the *Times-Picayune*, which had dismissed Slim's own murder with a little filler squib way back in the Metro section, saw fit to run the snitch's story big. That had hurt Ms. Linda more than anything. She wouldn't leave her house for days out of shame; couldn't show herself to the neighbors. Finally, a woman from her grieving council, who'd lost her son the same way, came by and raised her up. But she wasn't over it, still to this day.

So many things hurt. When Slim was still lying where he was killed, before she'd even got the call that he had been shot, one of his boyz, so-called, had stolen the Rolex off his wrist. All his jewelry had disappeared. Then others in Cut Throat Committy had asked for permission to go upstairs, where Slim had his studio, to collect their clothes, and they'd taken all of Slim's clothes while they were at it, even his tennises, as well as the laptop that contained the album he'd been working on. "And these were the people he trusted," Ms. Linda said. "He gave them everything, a home, a place to sleep and record, all the money he had in his pockets. And now they do him like this. I'ma say it right here, they wasn't real." She paused a moment, controlling herself, and when she spoke again, her voice sounded scorched, a burnt-out building. "This man, he was so focused. He'd come through so much, a whole world of trouble, but he never stopped believing he was going to be this rapper. 'Watch how big I come, Mama,' he used to say. And they stole his clothes. His friends. He was lying there dead, and they stole the watch right off his arm." She paused again, breathed deep. "I want my son," she said.

The more I learned about Slim, the more he haunted me. I had a recurring dream that I was trapped in the Iberville again and felt him watching me through the swarm of bodies, and I struggled toward him, straining to meet his eyes.

Before he was Soulja Slim, he had been Magnolia Slim, and before that James A'Daryll Tapp, only son of a mother who worked as a maid in hotels and lived in Court 6 of the Magnolia project, in the Third Ward: MP3.

Third Ward—that spoke volumes. The inner city was divided into eighteen wards, gerrymandered political districts that dated back to the nineteenth century, and each had its own character. The Third was the heart of black uptown, its annals full of music and violence. Buddy Bolden, the first great jazz trumpeter, came from First Street; nearby, on Saratoga Street, in 1900, a black laborer named Robert Charles ran wild and shot twenty-seven whites, including seven policemen, sparking the biggest race riot in New Orleans history.

Latterly, the Third Ward revolved around its three projects—the Magnolia, the Calliope, and the Melpomene. It was also a stronghold of gospel churches. Sunday mornings belonged to suits and white dresses, church ladies in picture hats. The rest of the week, its heroes were dope dealers and rappers.

None of the uptown projects had a tougher reputation than the Magnolia. Before the city started to tear it down, over four thousand souls were banged up there. They lived according to their own code, with their own governance. Police didn't like to go there. The one true law was survival.

Back in the 1940s, the projects had been raised in the name of progress. Black New Orleans was always dirt poor, a labyrinth of wooden slums. Fire hazards, rat breeders—it seemed a sane idea to flatten the worst and replace them with bricks. The St. Thomas went up first, touting free heat and electricity, flower boxes in the windows. Nine others followed.

By the time Soulja Slim came along, that was a lost age. Nothing lasts in this place without constant upkeep. The city is built below sea level, literally a swamp; decay is in its nature. The Magnolia that Slim grew up in was a dung-colored warren rotting on its foundations.

He was born September 9, 1978. That made him a Virgo, along with Mother Teresa, Greta Garbo, and Ivan the Terrible. Like most rappers, he took astrology to heart, always keeping one eye on the stars.

According to his mother, who called him Daryll, he was a quiet boy, didn't like to talk too much, though he was never shy. A natural-born hustler, he had a knack for drawing likenesses, able to reproduce anything he saw on TV. His specialties were Tweety Pie and Bugs Bunny. By the time he was in fourth grade, he'd turned them into his first business. He used to drawn Looney Toons characters on denim jeans and jackets, even sneakers. Every day after school, kids would come by the apartment on Court 6 and drop off clothing for Daryll to decorate. When he wasn't busy with that, he tagged graffiti in the hallways, up and down the streets.

He had a passion for shoes. "That's all he did in school every day, draw tennises, never would do any work," Ms. Linda told me. His favorites were black Reeboks, which he renamed soldier Reeboks. And he had a taste for camouflage fatigues. Between the two, he had found his uniform.

By then, James's father was gone to Angola, doing twelve to fifteen years. From the age of seven, the boy was the man of his house. "He took care of me," Ms. Linda said. "I was a scary mama, used to worry anytime he wasn't in my sight. When he went to the streets, I looked for him; his mama needed to know where he was. I tried to protect him too much, I think, but he always went his own ways. He became a man very early in his life."

Already he stood apart. He was tall and would grow to be six foot three, with a body like a whip and long, slitted eyes that gave off both menace and laughter. When you ran across him, one of his old running pardners told me, you never knew if he was going to joke with you or rob you. Sometimes he did both.

There was a presence about him, even as a child; a strength and stillness at his core. As far back as anyone could remember, he always seemed full grown. At eleven, he owned more than fifty pairs of soldier Reeboks. One way he paid for them was by cutting hair. This was a skill many rappers shared. Juvenile was a tonsorial artist, Mobo Joe and Lil Tee too, but Daryll was something special. KLC, later his producer, said, "Slim was a fool with clippers. He was nice with the hair-cutting tools." He came up with a signature style, the Third Ward fade. Every Saturday, his bedroom was packed with customers. He was in more demand than most professional barbers, but his clients didn't always care to pay, so Daryll kept a tommy gun next to his barber chair.

It was the 1980s, the city's economy was in the toilet, and the Magnolia was awash in crack. When the projects went up, New Orleans had been a great port, and the old artisan trades still thrived. Later, there was offshore oil. Now the port had been moved downriver, most of the artisan trades were kaput, the oil boom had collapsed, and major companies, beaten off by Louisiana's punitive taxes, were fleeing town in droves. Even if you managed to pull yourself out of your project and make it to college, opportunities were few. Most people with options got out.

The Magnolia became an armed camp, ruled by warring drug

gangs. For a boy trying to act a man, there seemed no higher calling than to be a gangsta—a G. There was no dignity in day work. Busing tables, picking up after tourists, hosing down frat boys' vomit and piss on Bourbon Street—what kind of manhood was that? But a G was something else. He earned respect. He lived by a warrior ethic—strength, loyalty, vengeance—and had a sense of belonging. "As far as what I mean by G-Code," said Juvenile, also a child of the Magnolia, "is the way we dress, the way we talk, the way we was raised. Tradition. When I say G-Code, I'm talkin' about what you went through where you from."

Young, black, and don't give a fuck. That's how O-Dog put it in the film *Menace II Society.* The trick for a young G was to take the world's abuse and recycle it into rage. You think I'm ignorant? I'll show you ignunt. Call me a thug? Thug this. It came down to pride. The system tried to take it away; being a G gave it back. Pride in your family, in your ward, in your own outlaw legend. And if you came from a project, pride in that project came first. It was who you were, it gave you a tribe. Souljas called that love.

Years later, in his last interview before he died, Slim talked to Black Dog Bone of *Murder Dog* magazine. Black Dog asked what growing up in the Magnolia had been like. "It built a nigga, bro," Slim said. "I'm Magnolia to the die, ya heard me? I'ma die with it tatted on me."

At thirteen he was out on the streets slinging rocks. "My nigga Gaylock, he a gangsta, he in the clink right now, but that was a lil G in the game," he told Black Dog Bone. "That was the nigga that left there and took me on a few hustles and all that kinda shit. . . . It was my first rock I ever sold. . . . I left there and sold it, got like eight dollars' worth of food stamps."

That was how small-time most dealing was. A few bucks in food stamps. If you got caught, you went into the system, and the system, once it had you, would never let you go.

Around the same time, Daryll started to rap. The Magnolia was a rich breeding ground for rappers. Juvenile, Turk, 6 Shot, Big Slack, Mr. Marcello, and Junie B all came from there. At weekends, there were freestyle battles in every court. KLC, the producer, used to DJ on the balcony in Clara Court. That was where Daryll Tapp became Magnolia Slim.

From the courts he graduated to local clubs like the Four-Nines and the Detour, where you had to be twenty-one to get in. Slim snuck in anyway, jumped on the mic with DJ Pee Wee. It was 1991, and everyone was bouncing.

Bounce was patterned on the call and response of Mardi Gras Indian chants. Its basic rhythm was the Triggerman beat, jacked from The Showboys' classic "Drag Rap," then spiced with attack dogs barking, second-line bass lines, and New Orleans funk. MC T. T. Tucker created it with DJ Irv and put out the first bounce hit, "Where They At." Within weeks, bounce was the only game in town, and it has stayed that way ever since. Every major New Orleans rapper, past and present, started out bouncing. Though it has barely penetrated the white world and you won't find much bounce at Tower Records, in the 'hood it outsells mainstream rap five to one. Rappers and producers wearied of it years ago, the same eternal beat, the same tired rhymes, but the street won't let it go.

Bounce is raw sex in dance, a music of summer block parties, of swelter. On Sunday afternoons, when the temperature in the bricks is around 110 degrees and the humidity near a hundred percent, DJs let blast for five hours straight and projects turn into giant mosh pits. Big fine women and slim fine women hog the spaces next to the speakers, action-ready in skintight shorts and halter tops, and shake that thing till sweat flies and the concrete underfoot turns slick as an ice rink.

The DJ calls out orders—walk it like a dog, walk it like a model, wobble in a circle, wobble out for me—and the women obey. When the DJ tells them to shake it on a stick, they bend over till their hands are flat on the ground, their asses in the air, twitching so fast they seem plugged into a socket, a blur of flying booty. "Now tiddy bop," the DJ calls, and the women raise their tops to show off their breasts. "Now show the globe," and the women bare their butts. "Now pop that pussy till the pussy goes pop . . ."

Slim had the skills for bounce; he could jump on any mic and turn the party out. But his natural bent was for grit and grime, and his real love was gangsta rap. So he came up with gangsta bounce. He went into KLC's basement studio on Parkway, close to the Calliope, and laid down titles like "Slugged Up Nigga" and "Soulja 4 Life." Then came "Get the Gat," hard-core thug on a Triggerman beat. It was his first big hit, not just in the Third Ward but all over New Orleans. He was fourteen, and the Magnolia loved him.

He'd dropped out of school in the tenth grade. For the last year he had rarely bothered to go to class. All he did was stand in the hallways and rap. Not that he missed much; Booker T. Washington, his high school, was not made for scholarship. "You wasn't no gangsta, you ain't been to the T, that's all," said Slim.

Ms. Linda couldn't keep him in line. She was remarried now and had a new baby daughter, Peaches. "I didn't like rap back then, it seemed a waste of time. When I heard he was up in the clubs, like the Four-Nines, I went to fetch him out, I did what a mama supposed to do. Then I heard him on the mic. Hoo-wee! I knew he wasn't playin'."

Between the clubs and the dope game, Slim was taking big risks. There was a desperado streak in him, a compulsion to push the limits. If anyone looked at him sideways, he jumped them, never mind if they were armed. And he was getting high on his own supply.

Twice he was shot, first in both arms, the second time in the chest. The bullet in his chest, his mother saw it all. "They must have been waiting on him two, three days, till he came out of the project. He'd just said goodbye to me and walked to the corner, and they jumped out and started shooting. I picked him up where he fell and started running with him, till he said, 'Mama, I can't go no further.' I thought he was gone right then but God didn't want him yet. The bullet went through his chest and out under his arm, missed his heart by a dime."

Each brush with death made him raise the stakes. "Coke and heroin, the uncut shit, I used to fuck with all that," he told Black Dog Bone. "If I see a nigga and I ain't got none, I'm takin' it from him. Give me the shit or I'ma fuck over you. That's how I was rockin'. I might be out there and jack this nigga this night and be out there at the concert with the gat in my back pocket, rappin' on stage. That's the kinda games I used to play."

The brazenness helped build his street legend. Each show he gave sold out, each new record outdid his last. Soon he came to the attention of Master P.

P—Percy Miller—was the one who brought New Orleans rap to a national level. In music, as in everything else, the city was far behind the pace. It missed out on the first fifteen years of hip-hop, didn't start producing its own stars till the nineties. When bounce came along, a rash of tiny neighborhood labels sprang up. Cash Money, based in the Third Ward, was among the most prominent, but even it didn't sell much beyond its home turf. P was the first to cast his net wide.

He had come out of the Calliope, named for the muse of heroic poetry, but got away early to California. Tall and lanky, he wanted to be a basketball star before he tore up his knee and opened a record store instead. Within two years, he'd recorded and released his own album, which sold enough to set up No Limit Records and bring him home to New Orleans a winner.

In 1995, when he hooked up with Magnolia Slim, P was still on his way up, the Horatio Alger of rap, already dreaming large. Not content with scoring a few fast hits, his vision was imperial. Before he (and Suge Knight at Death Row) came along, independent rap impresarios had been so hungry to hook up with a major label that they'd take any deal they were offered, however punitive. Not Percy Miller. From the outset, he insisted on controlling every aspect of his business. He financed and released his own records; above all, he kept the rights to the masters. No one was going to get rich off P but P himself.

Though he sold many millions of albums, he was a third-rate rapper. Skills on the mic were never the point. At heart, he was a businessman. "I built my record company like McDonald's or Wendy's," he said. "The customer is always right." His major talent lay in seeing through media hype and sensing what the streets really wanted. After the murders of Tupac Shakur and Biggie Smalls in 1997, politicians and the press went on a tear. The killing and thugging had to stop. Gangsta rap was finished. But the obituarists hadn't bothered to consult the ghettos or the white suburban malls. P did, and knew the demand was greater than ever. While much of the music industry cleaned up its act, No Limit went to the other extreme: maximum mayhem, fueled by tight beats; literally, a bigger bang for the buck. And it paid off royally. The Dirty South rose, with Master P as alpha dog. By 2003, one estimate put his fortune at $400 million.

No Limit's in-house producers were Beats by the Pound. One of them was KLC, the DJ in Clara Court on the nights when Daryll Tapp started rapping. Now he brought Magnolia Slim to the master's mansion in Baton Rouge, and P saw a potential star. "What attracted P to Slim was he knew that he was real as fuck," said KLC later. "That fed his ego because he had this young real nigga around him."

Real. For the pimps of gangsta rap, it was the holy grail. *Keeping it real, the realest nigga, real shit, real as fuck.* That was because nine-tenths of the stuff they peddled was fake. Most suburban fans couldn't tell the difference, just wanted a whiff of the wild side, but the streets knew, and Slim was street personified. "Don't think that I ain't no gangsta, I'm about my business," he said. "I ain't gotta put on a helluva front. I'm regular jugular, me."

At seventeen, Slim was featured on No Limit's *Down South Hustlers* compilation and an album was in the works. To signal his national debut, he upgraded his handle from Magnolia to Soulja Slim. Then he went to jail. "This is how bad my luck is," he told Black Dog Bone. "[The album] came out on a Tuesday, I went to jail the Sunday before. . . . I got busted on the lakefront with three guns and a vest. . . . They gave me five years. Thirty months, you know how it goes, I laid it down like a gangsta supposed to. Soak it up like an ol' gangsta. Nigga, if you cryin' in that bitch, you better stop cryin' in there and be a man."

He served his time up in the country, in Beauregard Parish, at the C. Paul Phelps Correctional Center. It was akin to boot camp, and Slim used his time to get off heroin. He did it cold turkey, and stayed drug-free to his death. "Jailhouse got me right," he said. "Eight years strong, clean and sober. I left that life behind."

His album, *Give It 2 'Em Raw,* came out while he was inside and sold strongly, considering he wasn't around to promote it. When he got out, No Limit was at its peak. Percy Miller of the Calliope had become so mainstream he was written up in *Rolling Stone.* "Survival of the Illest," the headline read. The writer called him "the realest man left standing." That made Slim laugh, but he made a second album with No Limit, *The Streets Made Me.* Then he went back to jail.

By the time Slim was free again, Master P's day was running down. His primary focus had always been on promoting his brothers, Silk the Shocker and C-Murder, at the expense of the rest of his stable. Now he was preoccupied with managing his son, Lil'

Romeo. Soulja Slim and his ingrate insistence on being paid what he was owed were unwanted distractions.

Years later, Slim still seethed. "I feel played like a muthafucka," he said. "I'm a real nigga, I ain't look for no contract with you. I'm fuckin' with you on loyalty. . . . I got some paperwork where I could try to go to war, but I ain't no nigga to go to court. I'd feel like an ol' pussy-ass nigga takin' him to court, ya heard me? I get it in blood."

In New Orleans, No Limit was supplanted by Cash Money, which had come before it and now ruled virtually unchallenged. The Williams brothers, its CEOs, were Third Ward born and raised, and their half-brother, Terrance, had run the Magnolia when Daryll Tapp was a child. But Slim had turned them down once, back in 1991, and wasn't about to retrace his steps. He'd had enough of being owned.

"It had to do with the older I got, the more wiser I got," he said. He still ran the streets, couldn't seem to leave them alone. His rap sheet included armed robbery and attempted murder, gun and drug possession, and multiple parole violations. But he was getting tired of the aggravation. He also sensed he was running short of time. Rap is a young game, and he'd been in it from a child. If he was ever going to nail the big time, he needed to get serious. "If we don't grind, we don't shine," he said.

He set up Cut Throat Committy, melting down the gold tank medallion he'd been given by No Limit and reshaping it as a razor. He went back to KLC, his first and best producer, and coaxed tracks out of underground stars like Sinista, Bass Heavy, and Dani Kartel. The result, *Years Later,* proved that the streets still loved him.

Other rappers, soon as they sold a few records, ran away. They bought a big house in some gated community and hid behind bodyguards, and the only time they came back to the projects was for a video shoot. Slim never left, except to do time. He might buy his mama a house in Gentilly, but he still came through the Magnolia every day, even though the city had started to tear it down and Court 6 was now rubble. "He loveded his project so much, he grieved and grieved to lose it," Ms. Linda told me. "It got to the point, I told him take a brick and put it on the front porch. That project was his all in all."

Everyone I spoke to agreed on his generous heart. He bought groceries for the single mother who ran short of cash, paid her family's bills, and made sure the old got their medicines. His own people saw him as a godfather, but the N.O.P.D. kept picking him up, bouncing him around the system. The day he talked to Black Dog Bone, he'd been busted again, and he worried how his mama would take it if he went back inside.

Even in jail, he never stopped working. "He used to do things to get put in the hole or solitary confinement because he could write in there," his mother said. His lyric notepads filled crates, raps enough to last him for years. *Focus* was the word Ms. Linda kept returning to after his death, repeating it like a mantra. Yet his urge to self-destruct remained as compulsive as his will to pull himself free. In his last months, there were constant rumors that he was raging out of control. One story had him pistol-whipping a man in Mississippi, another brawling at a club on the West Bank. Even riskier, he slept with the girlfriend of a local club owner and then mocked the man in public. That may have signed his death warrant.

It was as if he feared that leaving the battle zone would rob him of his soul. For every step he took to right his life, he took two back into the pit. His interview with Black Dog Bone was one long spew of braggadocio and threatened vengeance. Ms. Linda didn't care for it—"all that druggin' and thuggin'"—and told him so, and Slim promised her he'd do better next time. He was working on a new album with KLC and B.G., an old friend and running pardner from the Third Ward who'd given Cash Money its first global hit with

"Bling Bling" and thus originated the defining hip-hop slang of the nineties. "I'm 'bout to do it how it supposed to be done," said Slim. "I need a few million, me."

Then he was shot.

The funeral was delayed ten days while embalmers reconstructed Slim's face and body. Ms. Linda insisted on an open casket, so that New Orleans could pay due tribute. Unless he was seen in his camouflage leather jacket and soldier Reeboks, she believed, her son would not be fully at peace.

Thanksgiving came and went, and for a few days the chief menace to society wasn't gunfire but the aftereffects of turducken (turkey stuffed with duck stuffed with chicken). Rappers littered my living room, awash in antacid pills. In between farts and belches, they swapped conspiracy theories.

The morning of the funeral came in bitter. New Orleans is subtropical, a sauna most of the time, but when winter kicks in and a blue norther blows down from Chicago, picking up damp and spite as it crosses the swamps, the cold is merciless.

The D.W. Rhodes Funeral Home stands on Washington Avenue, not far from the Calliope. It is an area that once was full of thriving stores and music clubs, but it long ago fell into disrepair, and D.W. Rhodes is now a lone bastion of splendor: a massive, white-pillared temple to death, surrounded by blight.

When I arrived, shortly before eight o'clock, the doors weren't open yet, but already the line of mourners filled the wide steps and stretched down the block. Later, one estimate put the crowd at three thousand. I've never understood how these figures are arrived at or what they prove, but there was, by any calculation, a mighty throng, even though rumors of another shoot-out were in the wind. That was possible (a few weeks later, after the last rites of the much-loved Tuba Fats, Joe of Joe's Cozy Corner would step into the street and shoot a man dead for selling beer on his turf) but not, I thought, likely. In any case, it would've taken more than a vague threat of gunplay to keep the Third Ward away.

Uptown souljas clustered in posses, decked out in black Reeboks and camouflage gear, their jackets flapping open to show off their commemorative T-shirts. In recent years, these T-shirts have become a major feature of New Orleans funerals, especially in cases of violent death. Most feature a four-color picture of the deceased, with his dates of Sunrise and Sunset, and an inspirational slogan: *A coward dies a thousand deaths, a soldier dies but once; I'm gone home, but I'm still lookin' over my niggaz;* or simply, *He was about his fuckin' paper.*

A hero of Slim's magnitude rated more than one design. In the most popular, he appeared as Magnolia Slim and was posed in triplicate outside his project, with a large figure 3 for Third Ward. The jailhouse tattoo of the cross was visible between his eyes, he held up a Cut Throat medallion, and gold dollar signs framed the text. *The Streets Made Me* was blazoned at the top, and down below, *I See I Said, Jealousy I Said, A Fake-Ass Nigga Hated on Me I Said.*

In other versions, the usual Sunrise and Sunset were replaced by *Thugged In, Thugged Out,* though Slim's funeral wasn't restricted to gangstas. Every age and dress code was represented: babies in swaddling, old men and women in Sunday best, mothers and fathers, grandparents, even one large lady in a fluffy pink bathrobe and a Santa Claus cap. They waited, shivering but patient, as the wind whipped them raw.

I was accompanied by a couple of white acquaintances, visiting from out of town, and I also saw one white press photographer. Otherwise, mine was the only pink face, but no one hassled me. Possibly I was taken for a representative of Slim's New York record label, Koch.

When the doors opened, we were admitted two by two, as if entering Noah's Ark. Slim's casket stood in a spacious chapel lit by tapers. Souljas lined the walls, looking stern and forbidding, but the seating was reserved for family and close friends. Most sat in silence, though two women cried softly, hugging each other. Ushers kept the mourners moving in a steady stream, down the center aisle and past the dollar-green casket with gold handles, then out through a side door into an alley.

I had seen dead men in coffins before, but none who'd been shot in the face. The morticians had done a fine job; no obvious signs of damage remained. Neither did any feeling of Slim. Every corpse, dolled up for viewing, looks more or less like waxworks; this one seemed totally denatured. In the brief moment before I was moved on, I tried to catch some echo of the furious life the rapper had contained, his humor and strut and murderous rage, but it was all shut up behind the sealed eyes. Even the long, loose-limbed body seemed diminished. The figure in the casket looked like a shrunken old man.

What had he felt at the moment of death? Months later, I would read an interview with B.G., who believed Slim had blamed himself. "I know when it first happened, Slim was probably mad at himself that he let somebody steal him," he said. "He was probably like, 'Fuck it.'"

Could that be all? No terror, no scream? Not even a sense of waste? As I turned from the coffin, I glanced over at the souljas in their T-shirts. Many among them would end up on T-shirts themselves, young black men gunned down by other young black men, and take their turn where Slim lay now, amid the sick-sweet reek of incense and the dim light of the tapers, the soft weeping of women. Not one of them betrayed emotion. Grief led to fear, and fear was unthinkable.

On Washington Avenue, the crowds now stretched for hundreds of yards. Souvenir vendors worked the curbs, and young boys, seven, eight years old, walked with a slow jailhouse shamble, as if their ankles were shackled. I wandered across to the T-shirt store off Broad and ordered the Magnolia Slim. The youths in the store looked at me dully. In the street, a wispy rain had started to fall. A fat kid, paraplegic, went by in an electrified wheelchair; I guessed his age at fourteen. And I needed to get away. I had planned to walk in the second line—the mourners who parade behind the coffin on its way to the burying ground—but I couldn't see it through. The weight of useless destruction was too great. Slim in his casket, old at twenty-six; the children with their jailhouse shuffles; this fat smiling boy on wheels; and all for what? *Grieve at the birth, celebrate at the death*—that had always been the New Orleans philosophy. I wanted no part of it.

My friends dropped me home and went off to explore Cajun country, and I sat on my front porch, bundled in an overcoat, watching Lucy Ann, the little white girl who lived across the street, march up and down in a bright slicker. She was forever on a mission, that child. Came out of the womb knowing where she was going.

Three miles away, the funeral service was over and Slim's hearse, drawn by two white horses, was making its way through the uptown streets toward the Magnolia. The Rebirth Brass Band, dispensing with the usual slow hymns that started a second line, went straight to playing his hits: "You Got It," "I'll Pay Fa It," "You Don't Wanna Go 2 War." After a while, the coffin was removed from the hearse and carried aloft by his pallbearers, high above the crowd, bucking to the beat, as the procession wound through the wreckage of Court 6. All over the Magnolia, people hung out of their windows and clustered on balconies, and there was dancing in the streets. Then it was on to Mount Olivet, and the grave.

No shots were fired, nobody got hurt. According to Kayotic, one of Cut Throat Committy, the funeral was nothing but a love thing.

Love for Slim, and what he represented; respect for the soulja code. "Realness is forever," Slim's manager said.

On Solomon Street, I tried in vain to keep my mind on that night's recording session. I kept seeing Slim's face in death, and the image filled me with desolation. He'd been blessed with so much: energy and wit, a power over people, the gift of words, much love. And how had he used his talents? To boast of killing black men and fucking black women in the mouth.

The self-hating in this was terrible. What posed as defiance— *Fuck you, nigga*—had in fact been abject surrender. In facing down physical fear, Slim had bowed to the deeper fear of seeming weak. But humans *are* weak; that is our humanity. By denying it, we deny our own nature, and so destroy ourselves.

Who had killed Daryll Tapp? Soulja Slim.

And his story was one of hundreds, of thousands. I thought of the warriors lining the chapel walls, waiting for their day to come. The despair of that had driven me away. Now, against logic, it drew me back. A sudden rush of virus-fueled rage, more and more frequent of late, drummed me off the porch and into the street. I caught the bus to Broad, then got out and walked across the overpass toward the Calliope. After a block or two, the white world was left behind. The day was still evil cold and I had swapped my jacket for a sweat-shirt. Instead of a New York record exec, I probably looked like an aging doper on the prowl. At any rate, I wasn't welcome. A mean spirit was in the air, the exultation of the funeral procession gone sour and rank. Souljas passed me, moving in surly packs.

Near the corner of Martin Luther King, a drunk stumbled into me. Though no damage was done, I took it as a sign and turned my feet around. As I did so, I saw Kevin.

He stood a few yards up ahead, hanging with some friends. Though his face was averted, I knew him by his long, scimitar shape, his blue-black skull. I remembered how he'd stood in the street below my porch and asked me if I was married. "You're a happy man," he'd said. I wanted that to be true, so I walked up behind him and spoke his name, and he turned to face me. It was Kevin all right, but not the soft and anxious Kevin who'd called me Mister Nik. This one looked at me with open contempt. I was off my turf, an intruder.

His friends looked at him, not at me, waiting to see how he would jump. Kevin just stared, dead-eyed. It was only when I gave up and started to walk on that I heard him laugh. "Old white fuck," he said.

SWEET SICKNESS

The summer I was thirteen, I spent a week in London. It was 1959, and I was in love with rock 'n' roll. Elvis was my personal savior, but I was open to any music with a beat. Someone on a bus said jazz was good, so I went to Dobell's Jazz Record Shop on Charing Cross Road. It was a tiny cramped space, filled by would-be hep-cats with sorry beards. In addition to records, there were a few books. One was a Pan paperback titled, *Mister Jelly Roll.* On the front cover, it said, "He put the heat into hot music," and on the back, "In May 1938 the flashy, arrogant Creole, almost forgotten, but wearing a 100 dollar suit as sharp as a tipster's sheet, sat down at a grand piano, the diamond in a front tooth gleaming like gaslight. Jelly Roll began to play and in his gravel Southern voice he started to tell Alan Lomax his fantastic life story which reads like a Damon Runyon epic, overflowing with a fabulous selection of sporting types and situations."

I didn't know who Damon Runyon was, but I knew magic when I held it. Flipping the pages at random, I read: "The streets were crowded with men. Police were always in sight, never less than two together, which guaranteed the safety of all concerned. Lights of all colors were glittering and glaring. Music was pouring into the streets from every house. Women were standing in the door-ways, singing or chanting some kind of blues—some very happy, some very sad, some with the desire to end it all by poison, some planning a big outing, a dance, or some other kind of enjoyment.

Some were real ladies in spite of their downfall and some were habitual drunkards and some were dope fiends as follows, opium, heroin, cocaine, laudanum, morphine, etcetera . . ."

Yes, I thought. Of course.

It wasn't simply that I liked Jelly's style. At some level, I recognized the place and people he described. I had no previous knowledge of New Orleans, I couldn't have placed it on a map, but it seemed to have been waiting for me.

The text was enriched by David Stone Martin's racy line drawings. An octoroon showed off her cleavage in a doorway, a black stevedore lounged by the levee with a guitar, Buddy Bolden was brutalized by police, men with black caps and umbrellas marched in a jazz funeral, and Jelly himself stood in a sporting-house doorway, gorgeous in a silk suit and a panama hat.

It got better. On page eighty-six was a spidery map of Jelly's New Orleans, circa 1900: the French Opera House, the sporting houses of Storyville, the uptown honky-tonks and downtown cribs, Congo Square, the cemetery where the voodoo queen Marie Laveau was buried, and Chinatown (opium available). In the weeks that followed, I memorized every street and what had happened there, who turned tricks, who was shot, who sang the lowdown blues. Willie the Pleaser and Chicken Dick, Sheep Eye, Okey Poke, Aaron Harris (a man so tough "he could chew up pig iron and spit it out razor blades"), and Eulalie Echo, Jelly's godmother, who was a conjure woman—these were my new best friends.

I liked the pimps best. Sports, Jelly called them: "You should have seen one of those sports move down the street, his shirt busted open so that you could discern his red flannel undershirt, walking along with a very mosey walk they had adopted from the river, called shooting the agate. When you shoot the agate, your hands is at your sides with your index fingers stuck out and you kind of struts with it. That was considered a big thing with some of the illiterate women—if you could shoot a good agate and had a nice class red undershirt with the collar turned up, I'm telling you were liable to get next to that broad."

That would be me.

At the end of the summer, when I went back to my hometown in Northern Ireland, Derry's brick walls and rain-heavy skies seemed beside the point. New Orleans was where I lived inside myself. Every night, in bed, I strolled the streets of Storyville, a half-hand bigshot like Jelly himself, with my pistol at my hip and all those girls in satin and lace just dying to turn my damper down, whatever that might mean.

A family friend in New York sent me some of the records Morton had made for Alan Lomax at the Library of Congress, now re-released on Riverside LPs. The words were the same as in the paperback, but now they had a voice: Jelly's whiskey croak, broken by spasms of coughing, over soft piano chords. He sounded as if he was dying, and he was. Dying, and broke, and out of style. Still, he gave off a dauntless gallantry. When he unleashed those booming trombone figures in the left hand and the dancing, Spanish-tinged melody lines started floating over the top—graceful, elusive, shot through with loss—he was still Mr. Jelly Lord.

From Lomax's commentary, I learned that Jelly's swagger was not inborn. His given name was Ferdinand and he'd been a shy child, even timid. When he started playing piano in Storyville whorehouses, his respectable Creole family kicked him out of doors and he was never at home in the world again. Jelly Roll—piano professor, pool hustler, ladykiller—was the armor that Ferdinand used to brave life and its terrors, much as Daryll Tapp would one day hide behind Soulja Slim.

This made instinctive sense to me. From my earliest memory, I'd been consumed by a crippling sense of dread. The dread had no specific cause; it was just there. Some terrible thing was going to happen and nothing I might do could prevent it. Worse, this terrible thing was my fault.

In daily Derry life, I was an alien—an Anglo-Irish Russian German South African Jew caught up in the tribal war between Protestant and Catholic, equally unacceptable to both. That wasn't a persona I could accept, so I sought refuge in invention. Writers reshape the world to fit their needs long before they know they're writers. Thus, I arrived at school one morning to find that someone had carved the phrase "Unfit to Fit" on my desk. It was only when I passed fifty, remembering this, that I began to have doubts. Somehow the words did not ring true. I came to believe I'd carved them myself.

Over time, I constructed a front, clothed myself in arrogance and cool, and made a way in the world. Many people were fooled by me, and often I fooled myself. Not often enough, though. At root, I felt I was a fraud.

To feed the romance of myself as excluded, I developed two central narratives that carried me for many years, as a writer and as a man. The first was a fascination with and envy of male groups, of gangs. The other was the use of surrogates. Jelly Roll Morton was not my only alter ego, but he was among the deepest, and the nerve and grace I found in him never lost their healing power. He was proof absolute that there were worse things than fraud. Fantasy, braggadocio, myth—these weren't just fancy words for lying, but a sort of art. When in doubt, shoot the agate. And that was how I came to think of New Orleans: my city of beautiful lies.

I collected books on its history and buried myself in the rich span of its music, from Louis Moreau Gottschalk to Professor Longhair via King Oliver, Sidney Bechet, Papa Celestin, Louis Armstrong, Johnny and Baby Dodds, George Lewis, Mahalia Jackson, Fats Domino, Frogman Henry, Ernie K-Doe, James Booker, Earl King, Irma Thomas, and a legion of others. So much of my imagination was invested that I grew scared to test the reality. Twice I booked my ticket, twice I chickened out. Then it was 1972 and I was twenty-six, touring America with The Who and researching a movie that never got made. New Orleans (two nights) was on the itinerary.

The Who, already rock gods in New York and Los Angeles, had not yet fully conquered the South. Tuscaloosa went well, Miami too, but New Orleans was the acid test. We touched down to the sound of a black jazz band playing "When the Saints Go Marching In." A group of ancients, possibly culled from Preservation Hall, stood on the tarmac in suffocating heat. As we left the plane, the trombonist folded gently at the waist and slid to the ground, where he gave a couple of twitches and lay motionless, while the rest of the band kept playing. I asked the white man in a blazer who stepped forward to greet us if the trombonist was all right. "What do *you* think?" he said with a toothpaste smile, and ushered us into the terminal.

Worse followed. The chartered-bus ride into the city took us along Airline Highway, an endless succession of pawnshops and hot-sheet motels, backed by street after street of ranch-style brick bungalows. Then came Tulane Avenue—bail bondsmen, fast food, weed-infested parking lots. The Superdome loomed, a concrete mushroom cloud, and when at last we reached our hotel, it was a pseudo-Greek temple with the soul of a Ramada Inn. Ill-favored women in hot pants awaited our sexual pleasure. The bar reeked of Raid. Dusk gathered, and I got hideous drunk.

The last thing I remember is singing "My Prayer." It must have been late, after The Who's show, and we were in a nightclub. A blonde in a white ball gown was singing good old good ones and I jumped up on stage, grabbed the mic from her in mid-trill, and howled. I knew that I sounded grotesque but couldn't stop myself. I howled and howled, and the audience sat and stared, enjoying the wreck, until Keith Moon—a merciful man when the spirit took him—came to my rescue and commandeered the drums, turning fiasco into high-camp vaudeville, a communal singalong:

You'll Always Be There
At The End
Of
My
Prayer.

Next morning, I woke up on a bathroom floor, washed clean. It was a lovely day and the morning air, drifting off the Mississippi, had a sweet sharp tang. I collected Pete Townshend and Chris Stamp, one of The Who's co-managers, and the three of us strolled the few blocks across Canal Street into the French Quarter.

At the corner of Royal and Bienville, we stopped and burst out laughing. All three of us, spontaneously, cackling like half-wits for pure delight. Whatever we'd imagined or seen in movies, nothing had prepared us for this overload, every sense bombarded at once. The filtered, stained-glass light. Smells of coffee, damp bread, musky sex. And the music, so much music, some good and some terrible, all of it loud with life, blasting out of bars and Laundromats and passing cars, from balconies, inside courtyards, everywhere. "Fuck fuck fuck fuck fuck fuck fuck fuck fuck fuck," said Townshend, and I could tell he meant every word.

Tourists were few. Though there were some souvenir shops and a few too many dumb T-shirts, this was still recognizably Jelly Roll's New Orleans. We walked all morning and lunched at Antoine's. Nothing seemed to have changed for decades. There was a feeling of having entered another dimension, in America but not of it.

When Townshend and Stamp went back to the hotel, I kept on walking. I wanted to retrace the map of Storyville in *Mister Jelly Roll.* The old red-light district was long gone, torn down by the U.S. Navy in 1917, and the Iberville project now stood where Lulu

White and Gypsy Schaeffer once had mansions and Mamie Des-doumes plied her trade. The Iberville, still comparatively new and spruce, seemed a good place. I wandered its courtyards, feeling no menace. Men and women, porch-sitting, greeted me kindly; my British accent went over big. A man in a battered straw hat, who'd been in the merchant navy and said he almost went to Europe once himself, shared his joint with me. When I asked what I owed, he was offended.

I rambled all afternoon, exploring the backstreets and run-down neighborhoods that ringed the French Quarter. I'd never seen such beauty in a town: the wooden houses with their faded paintwork, the high shuttered windows, the stone stoops hollowed by generations of feet, the little corner bars, the subtropical jungles of blossom. My whole chemistry seemed altered, so that I saw with different eyes, and gradually I came to understand the reason: I was underwater. The fact that New Orleans was built on swamp, below sea level, wasn't just a notion; it changed every per-ception. The air had a velvet weight, the light was thick with shift-ing currents. I'd lost all gravitational pull. All I could do was drift with the tide.

In the end, I washed up at St. Louis Cemetery Number 1, the city of the dead where Marie Laveau is buried. It was badly neglected then, before the bus tours and graveyard guides, and most of the tombs looked like Piranesi ruins. Some of the vaults were virtual mansions, some hovels, some set into the outer walls like Dutch ovens—a necropolis of marble and crumbling brick, its pathways littered with beer cans, empty bottles of Thunderbird, and dime-store religious relics. Apart from a few drunks, it was deserted.

Marie Laveau's grave was covered with crayoned crosses and hieroglyphs beseeching favor. In death, the voodoo queen had become a patron saint of losers: gamblers, wronged lovers, the used and abused. Someone had laid a grouping of twigs with peeled bark at the foot of her tomb, the sticks crisscrossed in a curious pattern that clearly held some arcane significance, and I asked one of the drunks if he knew what the pattern meant.

"Give me a dollar," he said, and I paid up. Then the drunk swung his right leg in a swift, well-balanced arc—he must have been an athlete in his day—and kicked the twigs to kingdom come. "Stupidity," he told me.

The next day, The Who left town and I went with them. *The caravan barks, the dogs move on,* I wrote in my journal. But not for long. A few months later, I was back for a week that stretched into a month, and after that I couldn't stay away. Everywhere else I lived in anger and self-loathing, doing harm to myself and, more important, to those who tried to love me. My need of fantasies was so acute, especially when fueled by drink and drugs, I lost all sense of what was a lie, what truth. In New Orleans, the distinction seemed irrelevant.

The moment I stepped out of the airport and felt the first prickle of swamp heat on the back of my neck, breathed that velvet air, all my furies washed away. A taxi driver told me once, "You remind me of my cripple cat."

I rarely went to the French Quarter anymore. After that first morning, it had never seemed so fine again. By the end of the 1970s, it had been taken over by regiments of fat white legs in shorts, and Bourbon Street was a barnyard awash in human swill. Frat boys and conventioneers ruled. At weekends, a man felt naked without a name tag: the Equestrian Order of the Holy Sepulchre of Jerusalem, the Clinical Symposium of Gynecological Laparoscopists, California Youth United for a Stronger America, Forward With Chevrolet.

Mostly, I stayed uptown. By the start of the eighties, I was spending half my time there and renting half a shotgun cottage on the fringe of the Garden District. Five hundred dollars furnished it, a hundred more bought a jukebox. Two blocks away, if I crossed Magazine Street and strolled the Irish Channel, chickens pecked in the gutters.

The more time I spent there, the more dangerous its allure. *Decadence* was the buzzword; *America's most decadent city*. But I was after something more convoluted. Beyond the mindless debauch that came with the brand name Big Easy—drag queens and masks and bared breasts at Mardi Gras—lay a deeper darkness. Something elusive and death-haunted, fatally seductive. Patricia Highsmith is a writer I value and *This Sweet Sickness* was my favorite among her books. The phrase seemed made for New Orleans.

It was sweet sickness, no doubt, that brought me to Willie Pastrano.

He was an ex-boxer, and not just any old pug—he'd been the light-heavyweight world champion and one of my childhood heroes. Back in the 1950s, he used to come over to Britain and tackle the native heavyweights. They outweighed him by many pounds but he always gave them a close battle, offsetting their greater strength by speed and cunning, sleight of hand. Sometimes he even won.

He was a thing of beauty, Willie then. He couldn't punch worth a damn and, even on nights when he should have won, victory was often handed to the local lad. Still, the flash of him; the spins and feints and double-steps, the flimflam, the sheer bravado. Years later, he would tutor young Cassius Clay, who borrowed largely from his style.

At the time we met, in 1980, Pastrano had been retired from the ring for fifteen years. I was in town to report on Roberto Duran–Sugar Ray Leonard II, the bout that would end in Duran's *"No más,"* and the fight crowd was holed up at the Hyatt Regency, hard by the Superdome. It was another Thanksgiving.

The day before the fight, the two rivals were confined to quarters upstairs, while we hangers-on kept sodden vigil in the mezzanine bar, overlooked by a flock of giant, papier-mâché turkeys. I was bored and a little drunk. When I heard that Willie Pastrano was in the house, I sent him a fan's note.

The man who responded stirred no memory in me. The Willie of my childhood had been a greyhound; this one was a bull. He'd put on fifty pounds at least, heavy in the gut, massive in shoulders and neck, and he moved with a sailor's lurch. His dark Italian face, which I recalled as a beautiful boy's, was a road map of nicks and scars, and blotched with liver spots. Though dark patches circled his eyes, his black hair was still thick, brushed up in a pompadour. At first blink, he looked like an Elvis impersonator, but rhinestone jumpsuits were not his taste. Instead, he dressed as a mobster—three-piece black sharkskin suit, Cuban-heeled boots, wraparound dark glasses—and his voice was a bullfrog croak. Too many punches to the throat had mangled his vocal cords. "I got that graveyard sound," he said.

That was how he spoke, all one-liners and epigrams, part New Orleans street talk, part old hipster slang, part garbled blues lyrics. All afternoon and into the evening, we sat under the giant turkeys and drank, and Willie laid his life in my lap, ranging back and forth through the years. Sometimes he was a fat kid on Elysian Fields, sometimes a champ, sometimes a washed-up bum. He was at an orgy in Miami, won the world title in Las Vegas, lost it in New York. Relived fights, punch by punch, from thirty years back. Fucked Jake LaMotta's wife and worked for mobsters. He'd done terrible things, things he could never confess to any man. "Don't start me to talking, I might tell everything I know," he said, quoting Sonny Boy Williamson, and promptly spilled his guts. *Start* him talking? It was impossible to stop him.

We ran together for almost two years. After I moved into the shotgun uptown, Willie came over often. He'd sink into the overstuffed sofa, and drink, and lust after Andrea, my girl. "Can I be her little dog while the big dog's gone?" he asked me once, when I had to leave town for a spell.

Groups of tourists plodded past the front door; the backyard was clustered with jasmine and we had our own magnolia tree. Well, shrub. "Isn't it grandiose?" said Andrea, but Willie wasn't impressed. In his view, I was making myself too visible. No good ever came of raising your head above the trenches. He himself stayed in suburban Metairie, unseen. He and DeeDee, his second wife, rented a series of brick ranch-styles, more or less inter-changeable. Each time they moved, Willie hinted that he'd out-foxed the hounds of hell. Maybe he had.

Much of our time together was pleasure. Willie was a funny man when he wanted to be, and he could be tender. He called me Nicky, a name I normally loathed, but it sounded right in his ravaged voice: "How you makin', Nicky baby?" he'd croak, and cuff me lightly with a great paw. He even played the wise uncle. "Don't kill yourself," he told me. "It's got no class."

Even so, our relations were never light. Both junkies struggling to stay clean, we fed each other's self-disgust. Fighters must know how to sniff out weakness, to prey on vanities, or they don't sur-vive. "Something's wrong with you, baby. You got an evil stranger in your midst," Willie used to tell me, and I was secretly flattered.

I planned to write his life story, and Willie gave gracious con-sent. Most days he'd come to my house around noon and I asked questions while he drank a bottle of Mateus Rosé. When the bottle was empty, the tape recorder went off and we headed out into the city, retracing his history. His was a New Orleans I didn't know, a far stretch from Dixie romance. No wrought-iron balconies or shadowy Creole courtyards, no steamboats on the Mississippi. *Magnolia shit,* Willie called all that.

His home turf was downtown, the Faubourg Marigny. In the last twenty years, many of his stomping grounds have been gentrified, and there are designer coffee shops and gay guest houses now. When Willie gave me the guided tour in his ancient Chevy, it was all broken sidewalks and derelict homes.

His born name was Wilfred Raleigh Pastrano, and he'd been born in Grand Isle, Louisiana, the site of Kate Chopin's *The Awakening*. Martharina, his mother, was part Cajun, part Tchoupitoulas Indian. When Willie was a few months old, she moved to New Orleans. Her husband, Frank, was a ship's cook in the merchant navy. That made Willie, in theory, a Cajun Italian Tchoupitoula, but he had doubts. He'd seen his birth certificate, which listed his race as "Colored." When drunk, he sometimes wept about that.

Sober, he swept such thoughts aside. He liked to think he wasn't prejudiced; he revered Muhammad Ali and, especially, Archie Moore, and felt a warrior's brotherhood for the many black boxers he'd met in the ring. Still, there were limits. Once I walked in on him in the bathroom and he was staring at himself in the mirror, his face an inch from the glass. "Do I look like a nigger to you?" he asked.

When he was ten, he weighed over two hundred pounds, shined shoes on Bourbon Street, and other boys at Saints Peter and Paul called him Fat Meat. Afternoons, when he walked home from school through Washington Park, they'd hide in the branches of the live oaks, whisper "worms" as he passed below, and drop down upon him, fists and boots flying.

His best friend was Ralph Dupas, later a world light-middleweight champ. It was Dupas who took him to the hall behind St. Mary's and introduced him to Whitey Esneault—Mr. Whitey, an aged diabetic alcoholic who taught neighborhood kids to box. Willie lost eighty pounds, then put most of it back on as muscle. At fourteen, he was knocked sprawling in a street fight and swore it would never happen again. At fifteen, he turned pro.

He had skills and a nervous courage; he also had a nine-inch dick. He ran through the local fighters and many sweet convent girls. Too young to box legally in New Orleans, he moved to Miami and signed with the Dundee brothers, Chris and Angelo, the same Angelo Dundee who would train Muhammed Ali and Sugar Ray Leonard. His real owners, though, were Frankie Carbo and Blinkie Palermo. Two years removed from an altar boy, he was fighting for the Mob.

His natural weight was 175 pounds. That made him a light-heavy, but there was more money in the heavyweights. Carbo and Palermo started matching him with big men, wrecking balls, who ruined him over time. For fifteen years, his bosses kept him on the road. He had eighty-four fights and won sixty-three. He married and had five children. He cheated with any woman who caught his eye. To keep his courage high, he used cocaine, then heroin. By twenty-eight, he was washed up.

The Mob had no use for him then. Willie was shuffled off to Las Vegas, one step away from Palookaville. Bob Foster, the light-heavy champ, was in town, preparing for a title defense; maybe he could use a sparring partner. Then Foster's opponent was injured, all attempts to find a replacement fell through, and Sweet Willie was standing by.

For fifteen rounds, he fought from memory, skittering and grabbing, keeping the champion off-stride. Johnson, a murderous puncher, could never nail him cleanly. At the end, in a disputed verdict, Willie was given the title.

When the decision was announced, he told me, some power outside his control took over and lifted him into flight. Though photos fail to show this, he felt himself go up and up till he was floating. At the top of the arc he glimpsed a supernatural glow. Its force was so prodigious that it knocked him head over heels, tumbling back to earth. So that was how he was crowned champion—flat on his back, seeing stars.

He held the title twenty-one months, though his reflexes were shot. For $100,000, of which he got to keep forty before taxes, he fought Jose Torres in New York, and Torres destroyed what was left of him. From the first twenty seconds, he absorbed a non-stop beating. If he'd had any sense, he would have gone down and stayed down. But he couldn't make himself do it. All his life he'd feared he was a coward. Now, when he could have used a little yellow, he found he had none. It was the sixth round before Torres caught him with a shot to the liver that spun him around and left him draped across the ropes like so much dirty laundry. He slid to his knees, then dragged himself to his feet, clawing his way up. He couldn't see the crowd anymore but heard them baying. As he turned to face Torres again (and endure three more rounds of punishment before he was knocked out), his one thought was: *not in front of all these people.*

It was his last clear thought in years. Title gone, he went back to Miami and smack. He ran through his money, his wife and children left him, and all his teeth fell out. He went down to 130 pounds. His old connections fed him chump change as an enforcer. He did bad shit. The worst, he said.

One night, at an orgy, the girl who was giving him head came up for air. Look down, Willie, she said. His proud dick had shrunk from nine inches to five.

His employers found him unreliable. They thought about killing him but, like many others, still had a soft spot for Sweet Willie, so they stuck him away in a mental home. He stayed three months, cleaned up, then came back to New Orleans with $23.37 in his pocket and got dirty again. He worked as a bouncer on Bourbon Street, robbed pharmacists and doctors' offices for Dilaudids. Months and years went missing from his memory. Then he was pounding at a dealer's door in the middle of the night, dying for a fix. The dealer let him in and told him to wait in an anteroom, but Willie never could wait. He had to see what was going on, so he peeked into the next room. The dealer and another man were cutting up a body with a hacksaw. It was slow, messy work, and Willie was in need. He asked for his fix and the dealer gave it to him. He had no works, so the dealer let him have a syringe. Willie looked down at the body. It was no one he knew, so he shot up and left.

He cried when he told me that. He cried a lot. But there was always a lurking sense of relish, especially when he talked about a contract killer called Juicy. Willie said he'd had the wettest mouth you ever did see. At any rate, they'd gone out on a boat together in Miami and done some work. *God have mercy,* Willie said, and started crying again. Then he took another drink, and laughed.

By the time I came along, Willie was approximately reformed. To support his new wife and two small daughters, he worked as a trainer in a Magazine Street gym, and he'd written twenty-four pages of his memoirs. The first sentences read: "My real name is Wilfred Raleigh Pastrano, and I happen to know the character, Willie. It's like being a Siamese twin. But I'm both of the minds at once. One of them drifts, while the other floats in small circles."

Our own book was going nowhere. Every time a section seemed complete, Willie disowned it. It wasn't his intention, I came to realize, that we should ever finish. If we did, I might escape him and he'd be left with daily existence—the liver spots and bloody urine, the Chevy that kept breaking down, the promised jobs that never came through, the dead weight of time. "Willie lives a very boring life," he said. It was the one thing he couldn't cry away.

I started to snipe at him. One night, I suggested titling our book *Nine to Five,* and Willie picked me up in his massive right fist and dangled me above the floor, inching toward the window. When I reminded him that the window was eighteen inches off the ground, he put me down. Still, he'd made his point.

For a few weeks afterward, things seemed better. One day he brought Andrea a bunch of white carnations, stolen specially. Then he said he had a friend he wanted me to meet. We drove to Mid-City, to a Cadillac dealership. The salesman had a wet mouth.

Juicy looked nothing like a Hollywood hit man. He was soft-spoken and polite, every inch the salesman. Though he kept spitting on me, I knew it was not intentional. All he wanted was to put me in a Cadillac Seville. I told him I didn't drive. "Trust me," said Juicy. "You drive."

Easy laughter all around. Willie slung an arm around my shoulder, keeping me close. And then, quite casually, he told Juicy that I knew about the time they'd gone out in the boat and done some work.

"I don't," I said. "I don't know anything."

"Doesn't matter," said Juicy. But his eyes weren't right; putting me in a Seville was no longer his priority. I freed myself from Willie's embrace and walked out into the steam-bath afternoon. Juicy was talking on the phone. I started strolling up the street. A few days later, I left town.

I didn't see Willie for several years. By that time, my life was much changed. I was past forty, married and frequently sober, and I no longer needed the things that had put me in Sweet Willie's way. Then, one day in the late eighties, I read in the *Times-Picayune* that he was going to be among the guests at a boxing awards show that night.

The event was held at a downtown hotel; I wore a suit and took Michaela, my wife. A tape deck was playing "Raindrops Keep Falling on My Head" as we entered, and the room was full of managers and trainers shooting the shit. Willie and DeeDee sat at a window table. His liver blotches were more pronounced and his color wasn't good, but he was essentially unchanged, the hair as black and profuse as ever, the three-piece gangster suit and Cuban-heeled boots still present and correct. "Nicky baby," he said, as if he'd seen me only last week, and drew me into a bear hug, equal parts Old Spice and alcohol. He smelled like he was dying.

"I'm sorry," he said.

"What for?"

"The contract."

"Contract?"

"Nicky," said Willie. "It wasn't my idea."

What wasn't his idea, it emerged, was that Juicy had put out a hit on me. He did not choose to execute me himself, for fear we'd been seen together, so he farmed out the job to an associate, a slow worker who had other matters on his plate and didn't get around to me before I left town. Willie had always assumed I'd guessed what was in the wind. When I told him otherwise, he laughed long and loud.

It was ancient history now; I bore no grudge. At the same time, I had no desire to revisit the good old days. Next morning, he phoned me early and offered to sell me 300,000 tranquilizers. That was the last time we talked.

Willie lived on for almost ten years, finally succumbing to liver cancer in 1997, nine days after his sixty-second birthday. Instead of going to his funeral, I marked the day by playing some of the tapes from our aborted book. At the bottom of the box in which they were stored was a page from his memoir. One paragraph only, but all of Sweet Willie was in it, and what he'd been for me:

"There once was a beautiful, black-eyed little darling called Anita Russo down in Miami and I had it bad for her. She was a stripper or exotic dancer at the age of 12. Later, at 15, a full-fledged prostitute. She was then, at 18 or 19, a paid-for Lady Love. I never thought of women paying women for their company. But why not? Rocky Marciano ran her down to me. Finger popping, built beautiful, bust sticking straight out and real dark complexioned. Her hair was jet black and down to her ass—Lord, I dug her peaches. I called her Tee Na Na. Then she fell victim to the great white horse, heroin. A couple of black dealers gave her the stuff in a hotel room. After she died, they had sex with her. She had the softest touch my body ever felt and I'll never forget her, or the drug that killed her."

*   *   *

Beyond the matter of Juicy and the contract, the night at the awards show had opened my eyes. The city's nature was shifting, but I hadn't noticed till then. The fight-game characters, loud and gamy, who'd thronged the hotel belonged to a dying world, and the staff looked on them with open disdain. They stood for a New Orleans that was now surplus to requirements.

The watershed year, I came to realize, had been 1984, when New Orleans staged the World's Fair at enormous expense and hardly anyone showed up. As a result, the city as a whole was bankrupted, though a select few machinators got very wealthy. There was a blueprint here.

From then on, New Orleans became essentially a tourist town. Year by year, the French Quarter was turned into a Creole Disneyland. Shopping malls, convention centers, casinos, and themed museums kept springing up, each enriching the power elite. Old white money and new black money thrived. Meanwhile, the populace at large was left to rot. As the white bourgeoisie took off for the suburbs, north across Lake Pontchartrain to Covington, or west to Jefferson Parish and the feudal reign of Sheriff Harry Lee, the population shrank from 1.2 million to less than half that. While Houston and Atlanta, its obvious rivals, boomed, New Orleans became a backwater: one of the poorest cities in America.

Over sixty percent of Orleans Parish was African-American, as were the mayors and the large majority of the city council, so you couldn't blame it all on racism. Hundreds of millions of tourist dollars poured in every year, billions over time, but not a dime ever seemed to reach the streets, and black rip-off artists proved as adept as white. Over half the black population lived below the poverty line. The old neighborhoods, already failing when I saw them first, sank deeper and deeper into ruin. Dryades and Broad and St. Bernard, boulevards that had once teemed with energy, were systematically trashed, and the projects became killing fields. By 2000, the annual murder roll would be eight times that of New York.

More and more, I found myself disenchanted. I still returned every year to see old friends and to eat, but no longer kept a home. I was just another tourist now, hooked on that magnolia shit. I even wrote travel articles along those lines, and pretty purple they were—"Backstreets riotous with azalea and oleander, tea-olive, jasmine . . . clapboard Creole cottages . . . scented bayou somnolence . . . and then, of course, the food—sweet suffering mother of us all, that food!". But my heart wasn't in it. The streets were lovely to look at, the air no less velvet, the gumbo and po'boys as fine as ever. None of it was enough to compensate for what had been lost.

When I revisited old stomping grounds, I found them putrid with hate. In the past, one of the city's great attractions had been its openness, the feeling of mutual tolerance. Like all ports, New Orleans was cosmopolitan, a melting pot. Free men and women of color had lived and thrived here since long before the Civil War; there was a Creole aristocracy and a black bourgeoisie when Jelly Roll Morton was a child. Whatever racial tensions existed, there was interaction. Black musicians played with white; black and white neighbors gossiped over the fence. The races, in general, rubbed along.

Not anymore. Many young black musicians now refused to play with their white counterparts; white friends of mine were robbed at gunpoint, beaten, shot at. Statistically, it was a drop in the bucket compared to black-on-black crime, yet it changed the climate. The Big Easy was easy no longer.

By the 1990s, I thought of New Orleans as the lover I could never be free of. She might be faithless and dangerous, no mortal good for me, and I might promise a hundred times to quit her—I'd always come crawling back. Even so, my love felt soured, the familiar rituals stale.

It took hepatitis to rekindle the spark. In younger days, I had often played chicken with death or used health scares as a pretext for cheap theatrics. Hep C was different. Its symptoms and side effects—insomnia, exhaustion, psoriasis, vitiligo—were utterly unromantic, and so were cirrhosis and liver cancer, its frequent sequels. There was no drama to be milked, just the business of daily management. There were also compensations. Heightened awareness that time was tight forced me to stop playing games. My need of fantasy fell away, dead skin. Reality, by contrast, had never seemed so vivid or alluring. When I left the New York doctor's office on the morning of my diagnosis and walked into the street, it was as though I were seeing the world for the first time. Every atom was charged, incredibly alive. I went into an Indian deli on Lexington Avenue and bought a sack of the basmati rice that Michaela likes. Turning, I was confronted by a row of large vats filled with different bright spices—cumin, turmeric, coriander, red and yellow curry powder. Each particle seemed distinct to me. I knew its weight and texture, its smell in the back of my throat. A man with a withered arm offered me a scoop of cardamom to sniff. The intensity of sensation almost knocked me to my knees.

I felt I had been granted a second life. Whatever time remained to me, one year or ten or twenty, I must use for discovery. My curiosity, always large, became insatiable; I wanted to hear every story on earth. That hunger took me on a long voyage, back to Derry and through England, retracing my beginnings, and it was a couple of years before I returned to New Orleans. When I did, in the late nineties, it was a new city to me.

All sense of jadedness had vanished. Everything—beauty, perversity, seduction, risk—came at me fresh. I walked the same streets I'd been walking all my adult life and felt I had never really seen them before. The old neighborhoods were a crying shame, half the city was falling down where it stood, but there was a richness still, a deep secret enchantment that no amount of abuse could kill off. This, in the words of the old blues, was where the weather suited my clothes.

After I was swarmed in the Iberville, my wanderings intensified. I walked for days and weeks, searching for something I couldn't name. Sat on stoops, trying to coax some warmth from the chill winter's sun, and festered in corner bars. New Orleans had always been my spirit mirror. At every phase, it had shown me my deepest desires and allowed me to act them out. But those desires had changed. I was no longer in the market for beautiful lies. Dirt was in me that must be rooted out. It was time to be schooled in hard truths.

On a Sunday afternoon in Treme, the Money Wasters, a "social aid and pleasure club," paraded through the neighborhood. A brass band marched first, followed by the second line. Older men in white top hats and tails pranced and strutted, hemmed in by the crowds. Then came a DJ on a float, playing Magnolia Shorty's "Monkey on tha Dick" over giant speakers. As soon as he drew close, girls rushed into the street and started shaking their asses. When I had heard bounce before, it had always been at a remove, across a playground, down the street, blasting out of a passing car. This was the first time I'd caught the Triggerman beat up close, in the soles of my feet, in my gut and balls, and the effect was baptismal. The giant speakers, the steam-heat streets, the filthy lyrics and blazing beats, the DJ stoking the furnace, the girls in their skins—New Orleans was mother naked here, and I hungered to get naked too.

Next morning, when I sang in the shower, the words that flew out of my mouth were *Walk it like a model, I'ma do ya like a dog.*

MONKEY ON
THA DICK

I went to a studio on Banks Street, right behind the Dixie brewery. It was a grimy neighborhood, not far from the parish prison. The studio sat next door to an Abyssinian gospel church and suggested, from the outside, an automotive chop shop. The steel door was impenetrable; no windows faced onto the street. I waited on the sidewalk for Felton Langlois, who owned the joint, to show up and let me in. He was late. So were the rappers who were meant to be recording that night. It was April 2001, unseasonably hot. Sweat soaked my shirt and trickled down my legs. A beat-up Oldsmobile cruised slowly round and round the block. The man in the passenger seat kept looking me over. The third time around, the Olds pulled up and the passenger got out. He wore work boots and a Philadelphia Eagles T-shirt, and he was missing some teeth.

Some kids were playing Wiffle ball in the forecourt of the church and the ball got loose and bounced across the sidewalk. Without taking his eyes off me, the man reached down, snagged the ball and, with an easy flick of his wrist, dispatched it whence it came. "Don't be no fool," he said to me. Then he nodded and got back into the Olds, and the driver moved on.

The warning came too late. I was writing about New Orleans rap, a quest that had led me to Earl Mackie, the CEO of Take Fo' Records, which marketed many of the city's top bounce artists, including D.J. Jubilee and the drag-queen Katey Red, the self-styled Millennium Cissy.

It had taken me over a year to get here. For a long time, my pursuit of bounce had brought me only dead ends. When I tried talking to DJs at block parties or kids rapping on stoops, they saw an aging white man with no credentials and blanked me. If not for a chance meeting, I might never have reached first base.

One afternoon in the Seventh Ward, I was nursing a soda in a neighborhood bar when a middle-aged man in a dark suit that smelled of mothballs sat down on the next stool and started talking to me in a little girl's voice. His big body was lumpy and shapeless, a sack stuffed with mashed potatoes, but his hands and feet were tiny. He said his name was June.

He had been to a funeral, he said. He wasn't from round here, he stayed uptown as a rule, but a young boy had been shot over fifty dollars, a child no more than twelve years old, and he'd wanted to pay his respects. The funeral had upset him; he needed a drink. He started hitting the Alizé pretty good.

The skinny lady tending bar did not make him welcome. He had to keep drinking, pushing those dollars across the bar, or he was out of here.

"Where's your humanity?" said June.

"That'll be three dollars," the lady replied.

June told me he had trouble in his head. His brain felt like it was flooding with heavy water, he could feel it slopping behind his eyes every time he moved. He needed to go see a doctor. The street outside was as broken and rutted as a dirt road, and every time a car came bumping past, pounding rap on its radio, June got upset again. He was worried about his nephew, he said. That boy was running the streets every day, doing things guaranteed to put him in jail or his grave. June blamed that bounce shit, excuse his mouth.

Despite the little-girl voice, there was nothing swishy about him. On the contrary, he had a strong sense of his own dignity. He was living with a woman on Clara Street, had a job at Touro hospital. He was a provider, he stressed. Always had been.

Over the next hour, he told me the nephew's story. The boy's born name was Melvin but his rap name was Lil Mel, and technically he wasn't June's nephew, more like his ward, though considering how June had cared for him and raised him from a baby almost and loved him to this day, he might be his son.

Their story was so convoluted it took a couple more meetings with June and later with Melvin himself before I got it roughly straight. Even then, not all of the details tallied, but the basic tale seemed to be this:

When Melvin was five, his mother got sidetracked by drugs and couldn't keep him. He went to live with his grandma, but she caught a cancer and died. After that he was fostered out. The first family couldn't handle him, said he was too wild. The second family put him in a cage. They claimed it was the only way to stop his noise, so they shut him up in a chicken coop with a tin roof over it. They took the chickens out first, but not the chickenshit. When Social Services found out, they put him in a home. He was eight years old and he wouldn't speak. When he was a baby, living by his mama, he was never quiet. Chirping all hours of the day and night, he used to drive her crazy. Now he didn't say a word. The people that ran the home didn't know what to do. They sent him to a psychiatrist; it didn't help. They hit him; it didn't help.

The only person who could reach him was his mother's sister Maxine. She had a house on Orange Street, close to the St. Thomas project, that she shared with June. Sometimes she came to visit Melvin in the home and one day she took him home with her. She was a big fine woman with children of her own. Her children didn't want Melvin in the house, but Maxine wouldn't let them harm him. Once, when her kids were at school and Melvin was sick with the flu, she baked him peanut-butter cookies and they watched

TV. Then Maxine lost her house and moved in with a boyfriend. The boyfriend didn't want Melvin either, so June stepped up and took him on.

June had friends with a room to rent. It wasn't much more than a closet, but it had a window and a bunk bed. Then one of the friends turned ugly and started waving a gun about, and they had to leave. They moved in and out of different houses, and finally were placed in the St. Thomas. Around that time, Melvin started to talk again. It turned out he had a stammer.

A few days later, at June's suggestion, I met him and Melvin at the Popeye's on Napoleon. Melvin was eighteen but looked to me like a child, not much above five feet, and he was excited to be talk-ing to a writer from New York. When I tried to tell him I wasn't planning on a story, just getting acquainted, he refused to hear it. Publicity could jump-start his rap career, so he told me what he thought I wanted to hear—murder tales and drug tales—neutral-izing his stammer by talking slow and drawing out each syllable. Uncle June said the stories were lies and Melvin swore every word was true. They couldn't agree on anything, and finally June had to leave, take a walk to calm himself.

He wanted me to offer counseling. Maybe a man my age could talk some sense into the boy. Melvin wasn't bad in his heart, just ignorant. Didn't have the sense he was born with and he was easily led astray. That street life was good for nothing except to get you dead.

As soon as June left, Melvin stopped cussing and fronting, and ordered chicken with red beans and a biscuit. He had a raw-looking scab on his lower lip, the product of constant gnawing. A cheap faux-gold ring hung from one ear; the other was missing part of its lobe. As he talked, he kept touching the sleeve of my jacket with chicken-greasy fingertips. Whether or not he was telling the whole truth, or part of it, or none, it seemed to matter that I believed him.

June was cool, he said. Just because they went at it like cats and dogs didn't mean there was no love. There were men and even women in June's life who had used and disrespected him, and sometimes when he was drunk he got evil. He was never evil with Melvin, though.

Melvin had pretty much stopped growing when he was ten. He was in the St. Thomas by then, and the souljas there gave him a hard time. They used to whale on him, imitate his stammer. The worst was 'Rilla. He was younger than Melvin, but had a lot of gold—gold chains and gold teeth, gold shit all over him. He worked for some serious dealers, already moving up the ladder, and one day he backed Melvin up into a breezeway and pissed on him. Melvin went home for June's Glock and walked over to 'Rilla's place and shot him. He didn't kill him, barely winged him. He meant to shoot him dead, but he wasn't used to a Glock.

Life got easier for a spell after that; he had a reputation. Then June moved to the Calliope and Melvin was back in trouble. Calliope niggaz made the St. Thomas look like church. He had one good friend lived two doors down. The friend's name was Bobby Mabry, but he went by Bobby Murda. He was five months older than Melvin and built real big, and he had that winning attitude. Nobody messed with him. His younger brother Tyree had been killed and Bobby still had bad feelings about it. The muthafucka that did the killing had got killed himself before Bobby reached him. That was frustrating to Bobby.

June thought Bobby was a bad influence. He kept nagging at Melvin to do his homework and stay in school, maybe go on to college, but Melvin wasn't hearing him. Bobby was a rapper. He'd started rapping in juvenile prison, and everybody in there with him had showed him mad love. Bobby's thought, now he was out, was to make an album and a hundred million dollars. Melvin thought that was a plan, and they became partners—Bobby Murda and Lil Mel—and started their own record label. It seemed like everyone else in New Orleans had a label, why not them? Melvin suggested they call it Agent Orange, for the street he came up on, and Bobby thought that was cool. Now all they had to do was make a record, only recording turned out to be work. Melvin's target was to write a new rap every day. Some days he did—more often he got distracted. And Bobby was no help. Up in the clubs every night and high every day, and bitches, he never could have enough. Or he was in jail.

Melvin went on dreaming. Day and night, that's all he did. Thinking about how life would be when he hit it big, the Hummers and Escalades, and the house at English Turn, where Slim and Baby Williams had mansions and kept their families safe. Melvin had driven out there with Bobby a few times when they'd jacked a car. There was a gate with a guardhouse, and a golf course and landscaped gardens and a clubhouse with pillars. In the evening you sat on the veranda and looked across the lagoon, and all your neighbors were white.

The sleeve of my jacket looked as if it had been boiled in chicken fat. I asked if I could meet Bobby Murda. No problem, said Melvin. Then Uncle June came back from his stroll, and we changed the subject. June had treated himself to a sno-cone and was looking happier. "You make me so mad," he said to Melvin in his girl's voice, smiling in spite of himself. "Are you going to finish those red beans?"

Before we parted, I made a date to meet Melvin at the same time and place next day, but he didn't show up. When I called his cell, the number was out of service. I was standing at the corner, waiting for the downtown bus, when June got out of a car. He was close to tears.

The call had come in at three in the morning, he said; Melvin phoning from jail. He and Bobby had been in a bust-up on Orleans Avenue. Some juveniles had come out of the Lafitte and tried to rob them at gunpoint. Melvin fought back. There was a melee and someone shot off a gun. The bullet hit a woman on the other side of the street, passed straight through the flesh of her arm. That woman was fortunate.

June had seen the holes in Melvin's story right off. What were uptown boys doing on Orleans? And why did Melvin fight back? He'd been robbed enough times before to know how it went. A person steps to you with a gun, you honor his request.

He'd saved his questions for later. Right then, he called Cheapie Bail Bonds, like all those other times, but the bondsman advised him it was too late to get a judge, and Melvin would have to stay inside till morning. No big thing, June said. Those other times, when he'd managed to get Melvin released, Melvin never thanked him, just hit him up for pizza money. Heartache was all it was.

Come morning, he had traveled to the courthouse on Tulane and Broad. Lord knows he despised that place. Big old ugly gray building like some kind of fortress, they might as well hang out a sign, JAIL STARTS HERE. And how these children walked the halls. In the day when June was coming up, he'd say he was black and proud, but this youth now, they had no belief in anything. *Tatted up, slugged up, thugged out.* Even in the courthouse, they had to make an exhibition.

When Bobby and Melvin were brought up from the cells, Bobby had prison wear on. In June's mind, he should keep wearing it permanently, save everyone a heap of trouble. The whole affair was playtime to him, he never stopped yawning and flapping his gums, but Melvin was scared, a blind man could see that.

The judge set a hearing for six weeks ahead, so Bobby went back to the lockup. Not Melvin, though. June stood his bail and he was out on the street again, looking to celebrate. Soon as he got clear of the courthouse he started doing that gangsta walk, with his pants pulled down to show off his drawers.

They had lunch at the Cafe Verdict. June couldn't touch a bite, but Melvin ate for them both. This was disturbing to June. Melvin never ate like that; most times he barely picked. It was as if he was trying to be Bobby Murda.

What were you doing on Orleans? June asked him.

Business, Melvin told him, yawning. He acted so unmannerly that June couldn't stand to look at him, just upped and left him sitting. The trouble in his head was killing him; it might be a tumor in there. He needed to go see the doctor, he really did.

Soon afterward, I left New Orleans and didn't return for some months. By the time I got back, Bobby Mabry was dead and June was dying, and Melvin had received a sign from God.

June stayed in the Lower Garden District now, in a rooming house on Euterpe. After he got bad sick, he told me over the phone, the woman he'd been living with didn't want him around anymore. That hurt him at the time, but he was over it. He was with friends.

I went to see him the next morning. For many years, the neighborhood had been a slum; then it started to gentrify. Bookshops and coffeehouses opened up, new bohemians moved in. It was an old and beautiful area, close to the Mississippi, and it seemed it would be saved, but planners and real-estate speculators decided otherwise. A few blocks away, the St. Thomas had been pulled down. Suddenly there was a great swatch of prime turf, complete with river views, ripe for plunder. In no time, cluster-home condos in pastel colors sprang up. Now a giant Wal-Mart was on its way. Almost everything else was a mud pile.

The house on Euterpe was a tall wooden structure with a sagging balcony and some boarded-up windows. The city was going to pull it down this year or next, June said. He didn't think he would be alive to see it.

He had grown bulkier, the potato sack round his middle more pendulous, and his head was shaved. He'd been in Charity Hospital two weeks ago and the doctors wanted to keep him there, but he told them no, he didn't intend to be messed with. His friend Maurice, a stately man adept with herbs and powders, was looking after him. June had his own room with a TV, a washbasin, a leatherette La-Z-Boy.

His voice was so scratchy and uneven that sometimes I had to lean forward to catch what he said. The heavy water in his head made it hard for him to get around, he said. His balance wasn't good; he'd had a few falls. Some days there was pain, but he didn't want to talk about that. He was blessed to be surrounded by love. People brought him so many gifts, June said, with a glance at my empty hands. So many bounties from God.

When I asked about his life's history, he said he didn't care to look back. He had known good and bad, same as anyone else. His mother was still living, a righteous woman, strong in church. Although June knew she loved him, the way any mother loves her child, they were not close.

As for Melvin, he hadn't seen him in a minute. They'd fallen out over that rap shit, excuse his mouth.

What had happened was Baby Williams' birthday. There'd been a party for three thousand guests in the Superdome and somehow Melvin got himself included. To hear that boy talk, Baby and him were best friends. Anyway, from what June heard, there were a lot of shenanigans. At one point, Baby's big brother Slim had unwrapped a fancy Italian car, might have been a Ferrari, and Baby jumped on top of it, three hundred pounds if he weighed an ounce, and started bouncing up and down in his combat boots. Then he started yelling and throwing bank notes in the air, tens and twenties and fifties. Melvin got one of the twenties.

Later that day, I talked with Melvin by phone, and he fleshed out the details. That twenty hadn't come easy, he said. When the bills started flying, there was a stampede, and Melvin was knocked down and kicked in his head and chest. All he could reach was one note that got trapped under some other boy's shoe.

Melvin thought there was a meaning to this. He believed in omens, in dream books and the stars. You couldn't argue with fate, and Baby's twenty—to him, that was definitely fate. He was convinced it would bring him luck, but June called it gangsta money, blood money; the only luck in it was cursed. They fought, and Melvin went away mad. Then Bobby Murda got shot in the head and killed, which might have been a blessing. Even Melvin knew he was trouble by then, had started to keep his distance, though he went to the funeral and dropped a baggie of weed in Bobby's grave. After he'd taken his fill of food and drink at the wake, he went downtown on Canal Street and stood outside Burger King, eyeballing the big hotels. A woman with a gold dress and gold-streaked hair walked out of Le Meridian looking like a million dollars, with Juvenile from Cash Money in tow. Melvin watched the gold woman and Juve climb into a Bentley. *That could be me,* he thought, and he went into the Burger King and ordered up a meal. Paid for it with Baby Williams' twenty. Then he sat down and wrote a million-dollar rap.

In Melvin's version, that was where the story ended. I didn't tell him that June had already supplied an aftermath. The day after Bobby's burial, it seemed, Melvin had showed up at the house on Euterpe in a funeral T-shirt—one of Bobby's baby pictures his mama had picked out, captioned *Jesus Has a New Friend.*

He was after money, what else? He said he'd had a vision and wanted funding to make it come true. To turn his rap into a hit, he needed a backing track, studio time, and a bunch of other stuff—a thousand dollars, say. June didn't have that kind of money to waste. He said so, and they fought again. Some hard words were spoken on both sides; they hurt June's heart. His head got bad, and he had to rest. Melvin calmed down then and said he'd stay with him, and June slept a while. When he woke, Melvin was gone and so was the cash June kept hidden in a drawer with his underwear, close on two hundred dollars.

That, said June, is what loving gets you.

I think he died in the summer, though I can't be certain. The next time I was in town and tried to contact him, his phone was dead, the house on Euterpe abandoned. He'd never told me his legal name, so I couldn't check the official record. As for Melvin, no record was ever released in the name of Lil Mel and none of the other rappers I came to know recognized the name. Both he and June had simply vanished.

Vanishing is an everyday trick in New Orleans; nobody pays it much mind. When I asked around the Lower Garden District, I couldn't find anyone who remembered either June or Maurice. A woman pushing a shopping cart full of old clothes said I should let it be. If they want you, she said, they'll let you know.

Some months later, I met my friend Kate for a drink. She arrived in distress, having come straight from the funeral of Brandon Jones. He'd been a beautiful boy, Kate said. And others, later, said the same. Brandon Jones was a golden child. There was a light in him; just seeing him on the street made people smile. Everyone in Treme knew he was chosen.

When he was born, in 1979, Treme was an all-black neighborhood. Families had lived there for generations. The majority were poor, but many owned their own houses, handed down from parents and grandparents. These houses were lovely to look at, old clapboard shotguns and Creole cottages, though not so lovely to live in. Still, they were homes.

In the late 1980s, many of these buildings were razed to make way for Louis Armstrong Park, in hopes of luring tourists from the French Quarter nearby. The people who were put out of their houses to make room for the park were promised new housing in New Orleans East, a sprawling suburb of ranch-style brick bungalows, each with its own driveway and patch of St. Augustine grass out front. The promises weren't kept, and most of those left homeless ended up in the projects.

The hoped-for tourists didn't materialize, a proposed Tivoli Gardens came to nothing, a casino opened and closed. Though speculators bought up properties on the cheap and resold them to white gentrifiers, few of the newcomers put down roots. There were too many guns around.

Due to a bureaucratic foul-up, Brandon's legal name was Benson. He was light-skinned, almost honey-colored. On the streets they called him Red.

His mother, Regina, was sixteen when she birthed him and already had a year-old daughter, Tiffany. She was a riotous woman with a big laugh and an explosive temper. People said she should be a stand-up comic, but she was too busy working two jobs and wrestling demons. Brandon's father was up in Angola, serving life for four murders, so Brandon was raised by a rotating committee: his mother, his mother's friend Booby, and his grandmother, Miss Rose.

From the time he had shoes, he roamed the neighborhood. Treme streets were still negotiable then, you could use them to gain knowledge, and Brandon was desperate to learn. He was also saddled with an inborn sense of duty.

He was nine when he met Nan Parati. A graphic artist, she was one of the white newcomers, but she was here for the long haul. One day she caught Brandon smashing bottles in the street outside her house and told him to stop, because the broken glass had ripped her bicycle tires. Brandon was furious. Not only had she aborted his pleasure, now he felt responsible for the safety of her tires. He went to work in Nan's studio and she became another part of his raising. She taught him history and books, and he taught her Treme. He had never been outside New Orleans, so she took him to Philadelphia and New York, and to her family's home in North Carolina. Brandon told her there were mothers, moms, and maws. A mother said, "Brandon dear, get up"; a mom said, "Get up"; and a maw said, "Boy, get ya ass outta bed." By those measures, Regina was his maw, and Nan was sometimes his mother, sometimes his mom.

They had bitter fights. The mood in Treme was changing, and Brandon started running with the Sixth Ward Creepers—Peanut and Dookie and Fat Cory and UDog. Fat Cory had been shot and was in a wheelchair for life, which gave him status. At fifteen, Brandon had been shot at three times and could list twenty friends who'd died. He was arrested for shooting off a gun in the air, and again on suspicion of breaking into a car. That time he was innocent, but the cops cuffed him so tight he lost circulation in his wrists. When Brandon complained, one of the cops told him, "I hope they cut your motherfuckin' hands off." Then they beat a confession out of UDog, and Brandon was locked in a cell with a man who'd just killed his best friend for messing with his wife. He felt safer in there than he did with the cops.

On sunny days the Creepers used to sit out on some derelict porch and pose for pictures with their money and guns. That was Brandon's life. Then he would go to Nan, crying, and swear he was going to change. He sent her a letter saying, "I can't understand how stupid I acted for five years of your helping meracles that you gave me. I owe you so much first of all like a trillion dollars, my freedom." That, too, was his life.

School never agreed with him, but he could write. He started a hip-hop version of *Romeo and Juliet,* retitled *Homeyo and Ugliet.* The opening lines were:

COREY: "Chris who do you think is the finest girl in school?"
CHRIS: "I like Ugliet. That girl got the bigest tits in the world.
I mean that butt! When she's walking up the street in
the rain you can use her butt for an umbrella."

The arrests kept piling up, and Brandon felt he was going under. He checked himself into the Odyssey House, a drug-rehab center that emphasized self-awareness and taking responsibility for one's actions. Outside of weed, he didn't use drugs, but he needed to be out of his home, out of the neighborhood. By the time he finished the Odyssey's program, he had a new direction. Though he still hung with Peanut and Fat Cory, he snared a job bagging groceries at Whole Foods on Esplanade Avenue. In Treme, that made him a highflier.

He learned therapeutic massage, read any book he could lay his hands on, wrote poetry, and kept a journal. As B-Red, he also wrote hundreds of raps. With two partners, G-Sta and Casual T, he formed a group called Certified Hustlaz. Like every other click, they flashed bling for publicity pictures, but their music was politicized and self-aware, and Brandon's verses raged with a preacher's fire: "How many niggaz ya gonna kill before ya twenty-first birthday? / Is it because ya afraid to lose / Or is ya hood full of niggaz with something to prove? / Whatever it is, dog, ya gotta stop / Because you're quick to kill ya boys, but ya afraid of the cops . . ."

He tried to pass on the lessons he'd learned at Odyssey House: self-reliance, work, no alibis. Treme had become a prison to him. He was scared of getting shot and slept in a different bed almost every night. Another family now shared Regina's house, stealing Brandon's money and destroying his clothes. He kept working, and at last he began to see results. B-Red's live shows sold out, he was on the verge of a local record deal, and he was driving home from work with his friend Dewitt when a cop car came speeding down a ramp off the freeway and rammed them, killing them both.

Brandon Jones was twenty-three.

When I told Lil Mel I had no plans to write about New Orleans rap, I'd meant it, but Brandon's story changed my mind. I felt his life and death, and others like them, must be recorded. Nothing I wrote would count for much in the wider scheme; I knew that. Still, any marker beats oblivion.

At Peaches Records and Tapes, the primary source for New Orleans rap, I bought a glossy magazine called *Da R.U.D.E (Raw Uncensored Dope Entertainment),* whose founder and publisher was listed on the masthead as Loren K. Phillips-Fourous. I liked the name; it suggested decorum, a safe distance from gunfire, so I called her up and Loren came to my hotel.

A vision of elegance showed. Tall and sleek, she sported a turquoise minidress, cut low to show off a bountiful cleavage, cut tight to hug her hips. Gold earrings, manicured nails and a feather-cut hairdo that I suspected was a wig completed the look. Her hands, however, were large and her shoulders broad. Her name, I guessed, had not always been Loren.

Despite her stylishness, her street credentials were impeccable. Her younger brother, DJ Irv, had created the original bounce hit, "Where They At," with T.T. Tucker. He'd been shot dead just a few weeks before, Loren told me, and she was still in mourning. Her voice was low and whispery, her speech refined, but her eyes, exquisitely made up, were wary. People could be cruel, she said.

She had brought me the new issue of *Da R.U.D.E.,* which featured an interview with herself and an extract from the novel she was working on. We sat in a shaded courtyard and she watched me scan the opening of a chapter titled *From Behind Closed Doors.* The second paragraph read, "My most intimate encounters occur from behind the door. And I sometimes ask myself, 'Who's really the one in the closet?' From behind the door your boy who said, 'Man, I can't see me goin' that route, dog,' your son you raised in your image, your man, my man, now our man and sometimes his fantasies I greet without anyone knowing who's really the person on the other side of the door."

I skimmed the attached interview, in which Loren talked about spiritual values and the importance of self-love, and how she always set two plates at dinner, one for herself and another for humanity. How, I asked, did she manage to combine idealism with block parties and DJs blasting "Monkey on tha Dick"?

"Heritage," said Loren.

I was smitten by her. At this stage, my hunger to penetrate bounce was still undercut by fear, and Loren, with her hushed voice and perfect diction, promised painless access. When we took lunch together, she insisted on plastic cutlery, vacuum-wrapped for hygiene. "I have a thing about germs," she told me.

On a Saturday afternoon, there was a childrens' party at the Magnolia, and Loren took me with her. Her friend Goldie, a boun- tiful young woman with a mouthful of gold teeth and matching hair, was the presenter of a cable-access TV show that covered community news, and the two of them were going to contribute a segment on the afternoon's happenings.

The party, in the playground that fronted the project, was organized by King George, an uptown ruler who owned a hip-hip clothing store and a record label. He provided free T-shirts and food for all. However, there was no DJ, no bounce, so hardly any- one came except for a few social workers and two women dispens- ing condoms and AIDS pamphlets. Across Washington Avenue, along the frontage of the Magnolia, men and women filled the bal- conies, watching, but none deigned to come down, even when King George, a mountainous man, started dispensing turkey necks from a giant vat. Nearby, some of his rappers sat around a picnic table, looking bored. Big Slack, the first among them, was short and stout and wore a T-shirt promoting his new CD, *Ready for Combat*. It showed a death's head in shades and a military beret, over crossed AK-47s and the legend MESS WITH THE BEST—DIE LIKE THE REST.

When I worked up the nerve to approach him, I found Slack happy to talk. As with Lil Mel, the prospect of publicity overrode all other considerations. Before I could frame a question, Slack plied me with quotes and turkey necks. This was his first album, he said, and it was the bomb. "I been rappin' thirteen years, steady grinding, but I fell behind my business." Why was that? "Due to incarceration." Had he been away a lot? "Back and forth." Slack paused a moment to consider. "I'll be honest wit ya," he said. "More back than forth."

Before I had time to dig deeper, a small boy, no older than seven, came up while Loren, chic in a tailored pantsuit, was on camera. He had a walleye and wore a Rams football jersey that reached below his knees. "Trick bitch," said the boy. "I'ma let ya suck my dick."

Maybe Loren didn't hear, or maybe she knew better than to react. Either way, she didn't drop a beat. She finished her spiel and sashayed out of the playground, superb. Her flashy sports car was parked at the curb; Loren dropped the top and drove off with Goldie in the passenger seat. As the car disappeared from view, Goldie reached out a bare arm, scattering gnawed turkey necks like blessings.

King George's party, unfulfilling in itself, did wonders for my confidence. So long as I came armed with a tape recorder, it seemed, most rappers were more than willing to give me time. I didn't need a Loren Phillips to hold my hand; from here on, I could make my own way.

My next stop was Earl Mackie.

Take Fo's speciality was no-frills bounce, and its albums were interchangeable, a series of shout-outs and street chants, usually over the Triggerman beat. Whether the artist was D.J. Jubilee or Katey Red, Willie Puckett or Bigg Ramp, the recordings were always cheap and cheesy, and the samples hackneyed (the Jackson Five were a favorite source). In spite of which, or more likely because of it, I found the music addictive. None of the Take Fo' Superstars, as Earl Mackie liked to call them, pretended finesse.

They simply got up on that beat and let rip. A typical number would start out by referencing all the wards and projects, then progress to dance-floor instructions—*walk it, twerk it, show me what you workin' with*—and finish up with raunch. Much of the filth that I sang in the shower came courtesy of Take Fo'.

At the label's peak, in the late nineties, it was a power in New Orleans and throughout Louisiana, its influence felt even in Mississippi, East Texas, and the Florida panhandle. D.J. Jubilee, the Superstar supreme, sold forty thousand albums, sometimes more. Small potatoes by the standards of Cash Money and No Limit, maybe, but enough to pay the bills and attract the attention of Tommy Boy, a national label, which talked big money and tied up Jubilee for a year before deciding not to proceed. That had dealt Take Fo' a heavy blow, from which it hadn't recovered. Bootleggers were killing its sales. A hit album now was lucky to top ten thousand. "We had a window," Earl Mackie told me. "It shut."

By day, he ran his father's roofing business from a cinder-block building on Erato, a few blocks from the Calliope. Kids played in the street and workmen idled in the forecourt. A battered metal sign for HOME IMPROVEMENTS was half-buried in mire.

Earl Mackie talked to me in a small, windowless office upstairs, interrupted every few minutes by impatient customers demanding to know when that hole in their roof would be fixed. He was a large, slow-moving, moon-faced man, known to cling to a dollar till the eagle screamed. In all the time I was to know him, he never stood me so much as a cup of coffee. I liked him right away.

Earl didn't claim to be in the rap business for his health. He didn't even pretend to like the music much. He wouldn't play it in his home, even if his wife had let him, and he had certain standards. A Jehovah's Witness, he refused to put out any record that advocated killing or violence to women. Sex was different, though. His minister didn't approve, especially when it came to Katey Red, the Millennium Cissy, who rapped about cocksucking.

Earl himself had misgivings about Katey, but he held them down. "It beats killing people," he said.

His office was airless and fetid. Earl's bland expression never changed; he spoke in a monotone and his rare laugh was mirthless. Most of the time, he seemed half-asleep. This was deceptive. He had strong opinions and could be extremely articulate. He didn't believe in flash, that was all.

He'd gotten into bounce without meaning to. His family was middle class, his father the founder of the roofing business, and Earl had gone to college. While there, he and three partners—hence Take Fo'—started a cable TV show called *Positive Black Talk*. One of the partners, his girlfriend Nicole (later his wife), grew up in the Fischer project in Algiers across the river, and was bound and determined to change the world. Earl was down with that, but he always planned ahead. *Positive Black Talk* cost thirteen hundred dollars per show and earned only eight hundred, so he organized a fund-raiser. The theme was meant to be black empowerment; the co-sponsor was Celebration of Black Womanhood. Then T.T. Tucker jumped on the mic, and enlightenment flew out the window.

One of Tucker's hits featured the line "shake it like a saltcellar." Earl thought it might liven up the night to have a saltcellar contest, first prize a hundred dollars. Suddenly, black womanhood was all over the stage, celebrating by taking off its clothes and shaking its saltcellars. Though Nicole was not amused, Earl had seen the light. The evening raised five grand, more than *Positive Black Talk* could hope to earn in a year. "To my mind, that was pretty much positive, right there," he told me, almost smiling.

The four partners were reduced to two. Henry Holden, a technician at Cox Cable, came from the St. Thomas and knew the streets. They hooked up with D.J. Jubilee, also from the St. Thomas, and put out an album. It was 1992, and bounce was peaking. The album sold five thousand copies in a month, an astronomical figure for New Orleans. Earl Mackie was in the rap game.

For a time, before Master P and No Limit came along, Take Fo'
and Cash Money were the two hottest labels in town. Cash
Money's top act was U.N.L.V. (Uptown Niggaz Livin' Violent). They
used to play the State Palace on Canal Street, and Take Fo' would
counter by putting on Jubilee at the Saenger, right across the
street. "Those were battle royals, no doubt," Earl told me. Blood-
less battles, he added. Take Fo' represented the St. Thomas. If anyone started a beef, it would mean total war, the St. Thomas against
the Magnolia, Tenth Ward against the Third. Even Baby Williams
didn't want that.

If Take Fo' had started so big, I asked, why hadn't it progressed?
Cash Money and No Limit had both turned over hundreds of millions of dollars. I looked around Earl's office. A free calendar and a
yellowed city map decorated the walls; another customer was on
the phone. Earl shrugged. "Money."

Take Fo' had never had enough. Other labels (naming no
names) that were juiced by drug loot could dazzle new talent with
visions of bling. They flashed their Ferraris and Hummers, their
mansions at English Turn, their stables of fine women, and the talent was blown away. The record business, said Earl, was all about
a carrot and a stick. The way most labels functioned, they took
some kid out of the projects who'd been dirt-poor his whole life,
and they showed him all this wealth and glamour. So he signed
with them and made a record, and let's say he went gold or platinum. Then they owed him millions of dollars, but all they gave
him was spending trash, a few thousand here and there, just
enough to keep him in harness. If he complained, they acted
offended and said how dare he question them. They'd taken him
off the streets, maybe out of jail, and turned his whole life around.
They were family, they told him.

The family card, that was key. They made the talent feel guilty,
an ingrate. To show they cared, they gave him a new car or jewelry
as a token of goodwill, and sent him back to work. A couple more

years went by and everything ran smoothly, till finally the talent got wise and hired a lawyer, who found out they owed, say, ten million dollars. So they offered one million, take it or leave it. The talent was broke; all he had was some medallions and a car he'd probably smashed up by now. What's he going to do? He takes the million. That leaves the label with nine.

"The donkey chases the carrot, see, but he never catches it; it's always one jump ahead of him," said Earl. "That's why they call it the rap game—a game is all it is."

How could Take Fo' compete? Earl thought of himself as an honest man. He had no drug funds or secret stash. Instead of a mansion at English Turn, he lived in a decent house in Gentilly and drove a truck, provided for his family, went to church on Sunday. Each dollar he paid out had to be earned. Ten years into the game, he found it harder and harder to keep believing. Rap was about being young and hungry. Earl was thirty-four and studying for his MBA. He had, he reckoned, one more shot at the prize.

Maybe it wasn't too late for Jubilee. But Jube was Earl's age and his batteries were running low. When Take Fo' signed him, he was a substitute teacher, barely getting by. He'd gone to earning a thousand dollars a show, sometimes two. In New Orleans, where most people survived on a couple of hundred a week, that was *Lifestyles of the Rich and Famous.* Now Jube had a house on the West Bank, bought and paid for. He wasn't hurting. Rappers needed to hurt.

The phone was ringing again. Earl let it ring. For a few seconds he sat in silence, lost in thought. "We're still in the game," he said finally. Down below, an employee was leaning on a car horn. There was a roof to be fixed.

Felton's studio, officially called Smallworld but known as the Sweat Box, was a dark space full of echoes. An ancient sofa occupied one corner. Nearby, a wall was covered with the scrawled signatures of everyone who'd ever recorded there, and a short flight of stairs led to a door. Behind the door was the sweat box itself, the size of a prison cell, just room enough for the console, another tragic sofa, and a sound booth carpeted with droppings. I suspected rats but D.J. Jubilee said no, it wasn't nothing but mice.

He was a powerful presence, and a surprising one. Picture a rapper from central casting—the sneer, the slouch, the do-rag, the gun—and Jube, born Jerome Temple, was the opposite. There was a rigor about him, a sense of righteous self-discipline that suggested a drill sergeant. A lean, wiry man, his small head set stiffly on a long, hard neck; he looked as if his flesh had been whittled down to bare essentials. Almost the first thing he said to me was that he'd never used drugs, not even weed. He wanted to make sure I wrote that down. "Put it in your paper," he said. "D.J. Jubilee is not a fiend."

He liked to keep himself busy. He claimed he'd given two thousand shows and created over a hundred dances, among them the Shake It Like a Cissy, the Stick Your Booty Out, and the Penis Pop. When he wasn't performing, he was a special-education teacher and coached high school basketball and football. Like Earl Mackie, he was what used to be called a striver. Now you'd say he was about his hustle.

I had already been to visit him at West Jefferson High, where he taught. Most of the students under his care were extreme cases. One had to wear a helmet to protect him when he had seizures. Catching sight of Jubilee, he let out a rapturous squeal and started to kick the air. He had recently turned twenty-one.

Jubilee approached his teaching duties with the same showman's swagger he brought to a block party, even wearing his faux-gold Take Fo' pendant to work. Every student got a personal shout-out, like a secret code. He was teaching them the most basic survival skills—their names and addresses, how to count money—but made it seem like an adventure.

In the studio, he was a touch more severe. There was talk around town that he was past his prime. Jubilee had heard the whispers himself and was keen to set matters straight. It was true he'd been resting up, he admitted, but that was just to take a breath and come back stronger than ever. "The best and biggest is yet to come," he told me. "Put it in your paper."

When I tried to tell him I didn't work for a paper, he ignored me. "Write this down," he said severely. "D.J. Jubilee in the next year will be history in the making." Then he changed tacks. If his next album didn't take off, he might retire. "It's all or nothing, stand or fall. I'm done playing games."

There was a reason for his volatility. He believed he'd been cheated out of millions. In 1998, he had released a song called "Back That Ass Up," which sold big in New Orleans. The following year, Juvenile brought out a single on Cash Money with a similar title and chorus, and it became the biggest national rap hit of the summer. Juvenile and Cash Money claimed this was coincidence.

"Coincidence my ass," said Jube.

Reliving this grievance caused the floodgates to open. For the next forty minutes, he talked nonstop about his past and future triumphs, how he'd changed the bounce game and made it what it was today, how he was about to change it again, and how the new generation coming up had no knowledge, no respect. "Some of these fools, the way they handle themselves, it looks like they think they still in jail," he said, sounding less like a drill sergeant now than an aging fighter hounded by upstart contenders. He kept shaking his head in disgust, but his hard-muscled neck never moved.

The business of the studio, meanwhile, carried on undisturbed. Henry Holden, Earl Mackie's partner, sat at the console, his baby daughter asleep in his lap, and messed with a new beat. It sounded just like all his old beats.

Henry, like Earl, was large and slow-moving. He had buck teeth and a trick eye, no pretensions to style, but his smile was beatific. People loved him on sight, and he loved them back; he had the babies and baby mamas to prove it. This night he had come to the studio direct from his job and was wearing hospital scrubs. On Take Fo' albums, all of which he mixed, he was listed as Henry the Man, though he didn't seem at ease with the technology. "I'm not musically inclined," he admitted, twiddling at random. This explained quite a bit.

Altogether, the Sweat Box felt more like a clubhouse than a commercial studio. Take Fo' Superstars wandered in, bumped fists with Jubilee, and wandered out again. Henry's daughter started to fuss and was laid down on the sofa. The air quality was toxic, if pleasantly drowsy after a while. A rapper named Willie Puckett, one of Jubilee's back-up dancers, mentioned doing some work. "Let's make magic," he said. Henry looked startled, and Willie dropped the idea.

Through it all, Jubilee kept on talking, almost to himself. "Rap years is like dog years. That makes me an old dog," he said, and waited for me to contradict him. When I said nothing, he supplied the response himself. "I'm still the champ. They'll have to carry me out on my shield," he told the room. And Choppa walked in.

REAL NIGGAZ

It was 1979, a cool bright morning, and I was in Atlantic City at the end of a hard night's excess, walking the boardwalk with Joya, my girl, when a black youth pedaled past on a bicycle with a ghetto blaster balanced on the handlebars, playing "Rapper's Delight":

> *Singin on n n on n on n on*
> *the beat dont stop until the break of dawn*
> *singin on n n on n on n on*
> *like a hot buttered a pop da pop da pop dibbie dibbie*
> *pop da pop pop ya dont dare stop.*

I thought it was inspired—the freshest thing I'd heard in years—and started rocking to that "Good Times" beat in front of the Planter's Peanut shop. Mr. Peanut was not impressed. Neither was Joya, a black poetess whose musical gods were Miles Davis and Gil Scott-Heron; she thought "Rapper's Delight" was garbage. If this was what I liked, she told me, I had no respect for black culture and no respect for her. That's nonsense, I said. I see, she said, so my opinions are nonsense? I didn't say that, I said. Fuck you, said Joya. Then the kid on the bike rode by a second time—"To the rhythm of the boogie, the beat / skiddlee beebop a we rock a scoobie doo / and guess what america we love you"—and I started rocking again. By the day's end, Joya was not my girl anymore.

Years before, I had loved rock 'n' roll and written books about it, then rock lost its magic for me. As it took itself more and more solemnly, its power was smothered by bombast. The rock I cared about had been raw and hungry, full of righteous rage. Now it was ruled by windbags.

By the seventies, when I came to America, my interest in dirty old men molesting guitars was nil. The central premise of rock then, pre-punk, was that music changes the world. I didn't believe this, or not in any acid-nirvana, instant-karma sense. I didn't think love was all we need or that answers blew in the wind, and I thought "Imagine" was possibly the sappiest song ever written. The music I responded to didn't deal in fortune-cookie metaphysics; it was hard-edged and tough-minded, and it reflected the places it came from, the noise in the streets. The moment when something new came bubbling up from below, full of sex and fury, just before the music industry roped it and turned it into marketing—that never grew tired for me.

More and more, this came to mean black streets, refocusing a passion that had been a large part of my inner life since the age of eleven, when I chanced to hear Little Richard's "Tutti Frutti" on a coffee-bar jukebox and promptly became besotted with all black American music, so much so that my first pubertal attempt at poetry began:

> *Fats Domino Screamin' Jay Hawkins*
> *Arizona Dranes*
> *Swan Silvertones Sleepy John Estes*
> *Thelonious Sphere Monk . . .*

Cool names were part of the attraction. A deeper one was rhythmic. I'm heavily left-sided, so much so that I list to port when I walk and have to make a conscious effort to keep a straight course, and this dictates my reponse to music. Melodies in the treble— the right hand on a keyboard—come at me like verses read in translation. Drum patterns and bass lines, those are my native tongues.

What I responded to, above all, was how black music played with time, never landing square on the beat but slipping behind and around and ahead of it, eternally teasing. Most white rock, by comparison, sounded clunky. Four to the floor, thump thump thump, where was the grace in that? Even among white rockers, the ones I liked best, like Elvis, had supple, bluesy rhythm.

When black music was good, it cleansed. There was a directness, a bone-deep honesty, that seemed to me raw truth. Whatever its nominal form—country blues or urban blues, R&B, soul, jazz— at root it was always church.

For a time, I was that ludicrous figure, the white besotted with blackness. Norman Mailer tried to dignify the type as the white Negro (hip-hop, more truthfully, would call it a wigga). I never went in for soul handshakes or dashikis, but I certainly wished to be down with the brothers and sisters. Luckily, the brothers and sisters in question soon kicked that crap out of me. Which isn't to say that some taint of idealization, the flip side of condescension, did not survive their best efforts.

In 1976 my clubhouse was Othello, a black disco near Madison Square Garden. A haven for pimps and players and serious dancers, big style, this was where I first heard tidings of a new movement in the South Bronx. No one, as I remember, called it hip-hop yet; it was just *some other shit*. Nor did it get a big welcome. Many of the faces at Othello had come out of the Bronx. Acquiring the patina of disco sophistication had taken work, and they were in no hurry to jump back in the gutter. My friend Tu Sweet, a Hustle champ, said it wasn't nothing but a bunch of gangbangers acting rowdy up there. Sounded promising to me.

The South Bronx in that time was more than a location—it had become a national symbol of blight. Twenty years before, city planner Robert Moses had flattened much of it to create the Cross Bronx Expressway. Sixty thousand homes went under the wrecker's ball, uprooting 170,000 people. Instead of close-knit ethnic neighborhoods—Jewish, Italian, Irish, Puerto Rican, black—there was wasteland. Most whites, if they had the option, fled north to the suburbs. That left the wreckage, in large part, to blacks and Hispanics. Fire-bombed buildings, boarded-up stores, warring gangs—the same images recurred in dozens of magazine stories and in Hollywood films like *Fort Apache, the Bronx*. Fifteen minutes by subway and light-years from Times Square, the South Bronx was media shorthand for lost and hopeless.

That wasn't how it struck me when, to Tu Sweet's chagrin, I decided to take a look at *some other shit* for myself. There was poverty and ugliness, yes, but no sign of surrender. Every nationality in the Third World, it seemed, was simmering there; the air was thick with smells of African and Caribbean cooking. Drug gangs ruled many of the street corners and tenement hallways, that much was true, and the nights were lit by fires. Still, many of the new immigrants had come from worse, and my overall impression was of lives in flux, not dying.

DJs like Kool Hercules and Tony Tone and Grand Wizard Theodore were blowing up speakers in the clubs. Most had graduated from gangs—the Black Spades, the Savage Skulls, the Samurais, the Seven Crowns. They'd grown up in battle and seen comrades killed. Out of that slaughter, the survivors came together and started to build.

I had an acquaintance who lived off Jerome Avenue and knew the scene well, and he brought me to a club where Kool DJ Herc was scheduled to perform. When we rolled up around midnight, the club was shuttered and dark. Someone standing nearby said there'd been a problem about some guns and the gig had moved elsewhere, and did I have five bucks to spare? So I didn't get to see Kool Herc, the great originator, then or ever.

I did see other shows—a park jam in an uptown playground, a youth club near the Bronx River—and one rainy day, not in the Bronx but in Washington Heights, as I watched some break-dancers do backflips between the puddles, I heard the term *hip-hop* for the first time. I didn't know what it meant. Broken beats, an off-center rhythm—the basic drift was clear, but it seemed to go beyond music. When I asked the people around me, none could pin it down. Hip-hop was a style. No, it was an attitude. No, it was a party, was all.

A tall skinny dancer stood outside the circle, waiting his turn. He was Hispanic, an *indio,* with an eagle's beak of a nose. A raindrop clung to its overhang, gathered to a fullness, fell. Another drop took its place. "Hip-hop?" said the dancer. "It's the shits."

A quarter-century on, that's still as good a description as any. Everyone knows what rap is—that car with the monster bass speakers that pulls up outside your house at some ungodly hour of night and makes the whole block shake, to your great joy or deep loathing. But hip-hop? Over time, its nature has grown so complex, gone through so many seismic shifts, that nothing is clear-cut, if it ever was.

HIP-HOP IS:
A sensibility.
A global youth movement.
A black uprising looted by whites.
A lost cause.
A fashion trend.
A name brand.
A new term for money.
All of the above.

The ever-growing stacks of academic tomes on the subject don't take us much further. In Tricia Rose's *Black Noise,* for instance, we learn that "Rappers are constantly taking dominant discursive fragments and throwing them into relief, destabilizing hegemonic discourses and attempting to legitimate counterhegemonic interpretations."

Still, if hip-hop lacks a clean definition, it does have a narrative. To begin with, the story was quite straightforward—hip-hop was a street culture, and rap was its voice. The process by which this basic plot has evolved is, in large part, the pop history of the last thirty years.

In the beginning, in the South Bronx, the movement was a three-headed dragon—graffiti, break dancing, and rap. These, in turn, spawned language and clothing, and a physical style—a loose-limbed, shambling walk, a slang, and a warrior stance, the B-boy's crossed-arms staredown.

Initially, rap seemed the least important of the three. Graffiti and breaking were highly developed forms, each with its own recognized masters, when the music was still embryonic. The role of the earliest MCs was merely to hype up the crowds in the clubs and lend support to the DJs, who were the real stars. Kool Herc developed his trademark breaks—extended ruptures in a record's normal flow—to frame the acrobatic routines of breakers like Crazy Legs and Pee Wee and the Rock Steady Crew. Then Afrika Bambaataa added Zulu Nation funk, and Grandmaster Flash and Grand Wizard Theodore introduced scratching, backspinning, and slicing. Only then did MCs begin to emerge and commandeer the spotlight.

The South Bronx was never a true ghetto, shut in upon itself. The crowds at the first street jam I attended embraced black Americans, Hispanics, a wide range of Caribbeans, Asians, and a few whites. I saw some scuffles, and I heard there'd been gunfights in the Bronx River Park when Afrika Bambaataa played, but the mood overall was not aggressive. On the contrary, it seemed joyous—a feeling of shared release.

If there was a rallying point, it was class, not race. Hip-hop was being created on the fly, by and for the excluded, and its basic message was defiance through celebration: *We're here, muthafuckas. We're still alive. Check it out, we're more alive than you are.*

The *we* was all important here. Early hip-hop was essentially communal. Even Kool Herc and Grandmaster Flash were seen as partners, not remote celebrities. This was a secret society, in which every initiate had a voice.

The clothes were part of the defiance. They mocked wealth and conventional chic, reveled in mother wit. Typically, fake Gucci logos would be stitched onto denim jackets or sneakers, accessorized with outsize faux-gold medallions or glass-diamond bracelets. Mass marketing was held in contempt.

I'd like to pretend I took one look at all this and saw the future. In reality, I thought hip-hop was interesting, but not very. The park jams were exhilarating, and I admired the breakers, although a little of human pretzels spinning on their backs went a long way with me. As for the graffiti writers, I thought their cult overblown, especially after they became downtown art-world darlings. And the music? I heard it chiefly as an offshoot of Jamaican sound systems, of King Tubby and Lee Perry, not likely to have much impact on the mainstream.

"Rapper's Delight" changed my mind enough so that I attempted to write, at the instigation of the artist Jean-Paul Goude, a Spanish Harlem street film, set to hip-hop beats. Even so, I didn't recognize what others already took for granted—that rap was a revolution of sorts, the first truly new thing in popular music since rock 'n' roll—until 1982, and "The Message."

For rap, all roads lead back to this. In the course of its three minutes and ten seconds, Grandmaster Flash and the Furious Five, with Melle Mel on the mic, mapped out the hip-hop universe. Everything that's come since can be measured against the vistas it opened up, the promises it implied.

More than party music, here was a world: "Rats in the front room, roaches in the back / Junkie's in the alley with a baseball bat . . . Don't push me, cause I'm close to the edge . . ." And then, the Grandmaster's backing track. That cheezy little synth riff, rising and falling, as nagging as toothache, and the unbalanced lurch of the bass line, that spavined hip-hop strut—the perfect mad rhythm for a mad planet.

Twenty-plus years and thousands of subsequent ghetto tales have blurred the lyrics' impact on the page. On disc, in Melle Mel's blunt rap, they are as potent as ever. Other songwriters, such as Marvin Gaye and Sly Stone, had tackled similar subjects, but they'd kept an elegant distance, speaking more in sorrow than in rage. "The Message" was lived, every grimy, angry, suffering bar of it. When I heard Melle Mel's voice rise on "edge" and saw the grainy, home-movie video, it seemed the real thing.

Real. That hair-shirt word again. By now it has been so devalued in rap that, like *freedom* in politics, it has come to mean its opposite. The moment a rapper tells me he's real, my teeth start to grate and I check my wallet. But it wasn't always thus. Time was when reality was the core of hip-hop's intent, its one sacred vow. No matter what, it promised, it wouldn't lie. Then it lied.

Not right away, though. In "The Message," and through most of the eighties, it kept the faith. And it was fearless. The culture was inventing itself as it went along and rappers could say anything, anything at all, so long as they had the nuts and the beats to make it stick.

The best and worst about unleashing a form in which everyone has an equal voice is that ninety percent of humans, given the chance, talk rubbish. No, make that ninety-five. And, in hip-hop, the figure might well have been higher. Right from the start, it attracted the bizarre and the downright mad. Ten thousand tongues of Babel, all blathering at once; logorrheacs, sickos, verbal anarchists, clowns, and the occasional prophet. But all of them, and this was the magic, were fantastically alive.

By 1986, a second wave of rhymers was at the gates, and hip-hop came into its full pomp. The majority of early records had been variations on the formula of "Rappers Delight"—witty but repetitive boasts about the MCs' prowess on the mic and in the sack, chanted over seventies' funk tracks. Now, following "The Message," rappers reached for new levels of political and social awareness, set against more challenging backing tracks. Recording techniques had advanced, producers dug deeper and wider for samples, lyricists took bigger risks. Public Enemy and KRS-One, Eric B. and Rakim, De La Soul, MC Lyte and Big Daddy Kane, Run-D.M.C. and Queen Latifah and Slick Rick and Erick Sermon and Doug E. Fresh and Marley Marl and Pete Rock—here was magnificent delirium.

Watching from the sidelines, I found the spectacle of the music industry's contortions as rap began to take over almost as enthralling as the takeover itself. For a long time, the major labels had tried to turn a blind eye. The consensus was that hip-hop was a novelty fad, roughly on a par with pet rocks and lava lamps, and could safely be ignored. When it refused to go away, indifference turned to active loathing.

Many of the loudest naysayers were black A&R (Artists & Repertoire) men raised on jazz and rhythm 'n' blues, who felt profoundly threatened. Rap spoke for everything they'd struggled to rise above—ignorant ghetto shit—and they could hardly wait to dance on its grave. Apart from Sylvia Robinson at Sugar Hill and Russell Simmons at Def Jam, most of hip-hop's early backers were Jews.

The central complaint, from blacks and whites alike, was that rap wasn't music. You might think an industry that waxed fat on Olivia Newton-John and the Bay City Rollers would tread lightly around aesthetics. Then again, irony has never been the record business's strong suit. Its history, every time that something new and challenging rears its head, is to scream bloody murder and proclaim the death of real music. When rock 'n' roll was the threat, real music meant Sinatra and Perry Como. Now, under fire from rap, it meant Paul Simon and Billy Joel.

These panics are driven less by love of art for art's sake than by bone idleness. No trade is more parasitic than the music biz. If not for a few mavericks and iconoclasts, it would never budge an inch. Every time I walk into a major record label and see those bland, unctuous faces, oozing self-congratulation, I'm reminded of Dominick Corso, an old-time New York politician who stood up in the City Council one day, enraged by calls for reform, and said, "You think it takes guts to stand up for what's right? That doesn't take guts. What takes guts is to stand up for what you know is wrong, day after day, year after year."

Everything that made rap new and challenging was seen as a threat. To my ears, the fact that it ditched conventional pop form—the thirty-two-bar Tin Pan Alley song—was an enormous plus. What's so marvelous about regurgitating the same chord progressions and harmonies ad nauseam? We live in an electronic age, after all. Better one machine, inventively deployed, than a thousand brain-dead power ballads. Sacrilege, said the music-biz veterans; machines have no soul. More soul than Michael Bolton, I thought.

Only money, lots of it, could change the industry's mind. By the late eighties, Run-D.M.C. and the Beastie Boys were selling millions of albums and the major labels started to drag their carcasses aboard, although they were still not happy. I remember the convulsive shudder of a high-up at Atlantic Records when I played him Run-D.M.C.'s "Sucker MCs"—no bass line and no hook, just a drum machine that sounded as though it had killed its keeper and run amok, with the rappers, yelling frantically back and forth, in bootless pursuit. And there were unfortunate incidents—gang members going on a rampage before a show in Long Beach, California, or the Beastie Boys promoting a giant inflatable penis. Black community leaders had hated rap from the jump; now white parents were also outraged. A gunfight in the Bronx River Park was one thing, but one of their own kids could've gotten hurt in Long Beach.

Instead of harmless party songs or consciousness-raising, hip-hop, in the tabloid mind, now stood for anarchy. Soon Tipper Gore and her anti-rap lobby were forcing the industry to label hard-core CDs with PARENTAL ADVISORY: EXPLICIT CONTENT. This was the kind of advertising money can't buy. The industry should have given the lady a platinum thong and crowned her Tippa, Da Baddest Bitch. Instead, it wrung its hands and invoked the Fifth Amendment.

Since the major labels didn't know how to handle hip-hop, they started to make partnership deals with young, hungry independents like Russell Simmons and Rick Rubin at Def Jam, or Tom Silverman at Tommy Boy. Let them do the hard labor—discover and harness new talent, hype it on the streets, set trends. That way, they could take the heat for perverting the world's youth, a role most of them enjoyed anyway, while their rich uncles in suits focused on moving units and dividing up the profits.

By 1990, rap was on its way to becoming a billion-dollar industry. Predictably, this brought an upsurge in gloss and hype, and a sharp decline in political content. Teachers and preachers found themselves marginalized in favor of lightweights like MC Hammer and Vanilla Ice, whom the majors found easier to handle. At root, Hammer and Ice were pop idols in hip-hop *schmutter,* easy to market, disposable as Kleenex. The golden age, when rappers took big risks and carved out new worlds, was already past.

Purists began to refer to themselves as hip-hop heads, and a sorry bunch they were, forever bemoaning lost Eden. Introspection, poetic metaphors, pleas for black togetherness—the streets didn't want to hear it. More important, neither did the white suburbs. Rap's axis had shifted. Gangstas had stolen the game.

Here was the great divide, the end of rap's first act and the start of its becoming, for better and worse, the dominant pop culture of our time. It also marked the moment when my own attitude morphed from detached appreciation to consuming, though angst-shot, obsession.

If gangsta rap hadn't happened, hip-hop might be pretty much memory by now. The industry, having ridden pop rap to death, would have doubtless ditched it in favor of some newer fad, leaving serious rap to dodder along in coffeehouses and poetry slams and the halls of black academia. As it is, there are Golden Oldies' tours and a South Bronx nostalgia mill, churning out a stream of oral histories every bit as exhaustive as the reconstructions of obscure Mod bands and doomed singer/songwriters so beloved by rockists. Worthy stuff, but it whiffs of formaldehyde.

Gangsta, in large part, began as a reaction to this creeping gentrification, and to East Coast elitism in particular. New York, having given birth to hip-hop, had always treated it as a private preserve. No rapper outside the five boroughs could be taken seriously. Beyond the Hudson lay wilderness.

California, among other outposts, was unimpressed. It saw New York not as a mecca, but as inbred and effete, too busy pontificating to notice that the times had passed it by. "Everybody tryin' to do this black power and shit, so I was like, let's give 'em an alternative," said Dr. Dre of N.W.A., gangsta's new standard-bearers out West, "'nigganigganigga fuckthisfuckthat bitchbitchbitch suckmydick.'"

The idea wasn't entirely new. From the South Bronx on, hip-hop had always embraced outlaw codes. The difference now was one of degree. In early rap, the tough talk had been playful. MCs bragged about killing with their rhyming skills, not with Glocks, and the cussing was minimal. And this same playfulness extended to sex. Though every rapper was God's gift to womankind, he used wit, not menace, to have his wicked way. The keynote was flirtation.

N.W.A. didn't flirt.

Niggaz With Attitude. Fifteen years on, I still have muscle memory of the jolt I felt the first time I heard *Straight Outta Compton,* their breakthrough album, and realized what the acronym stood for. *Nigger*—that loathsome word, symbol for so much suffering—was the one taboo I'd have bet the ranch would never be broken. Now N.W.A. had picked it out of the ooze and slung it back in history's face, not merely acknowledging but reveling in it.

It was a stunning act of subversion. In essence, it took racial abuse and turned it into a boast. *Shiftless, degenerate, violent, dumb*—that's us. Black beasts, fit for nothing but fucking and killing. What you plan to do about it, muthafuckas?

Of course, it was a pose. That didn't make it less insidious. Gangsta was the tempter's tongue, luring believers from the true path. Forget about self-improvement and spiritual striving, it said, and get the money. Get it in cash, get it in goods. Cars and houses and mink coats, as much gold and platinum as you can wear without melting down. Though bling was not a word yet, its age had been born.

Like the first hip-hoppers in the South Bronx, N.W.A. made party music, only this time the party was hard-core. Used to be, it was enough to bring beer and sodas. Now you needed to bring your gun. Songs like "Fuck Tha Police" and "Gangsta Gangsta" set the new rules—macho chest-thumping, abuse of women, smoking chronic, shooting it out with other Gs or the cops, all presented as good times, a *nigga's* right to life and death.

I should have hated it, and part of me did. Another part, which I would have preferred to deny, wallowed in the mire. N.W.A. were very good at what they did, so good they could make me forget what they were saying and lose myself in the force with which they said it. Much as I respected Public Enemy and KRS-One, I was tired of being harangued. Like rock, hip-hop had fallen into the trap of believing that its job was to change the world, when its real function was to echo it. And the echoes I heard in gangsta—Ice-T and Scarface, even more than N.W.A.—excited and disturbed me profoundly. Anger, guilt, disgust, infantile glee, and a sneaking envy of the G's freedom, his license to say the unsayable—so many responses warred in me, I couldn't parcel them up in a simple judgment. All I knew was that gangsta tapped into something visceral in the way we live now, and in myself.

Black enemies of rap have often claimed that gangsta is a conspiracy of white corporations to entrap and poison young black minds, while white enemies of rap have claimed it is a conspiracy of black thugs to entrap and poison young white minds. Both views are nonsense. Originally, gangsta was created by blacks, often on small black labels, and aimed at a black audience. White teens soon took it up, at which point the major labels jumped on the bandwagon and phonied it up. This doesn't mean that gangsta was artificial from the start. If it had been, it wouldn't have packed such a wallop.

Even more than viciousness and misogyny, what made gangsta so troubling was its absolute absence of hope. Beneath the cartoon overkill, it spoke of a fundamental shift in how young black men saw the world. Years earlier, in the South Bronx and Bed-Stuy and Harlem, I'd listened while B-boys talked. Many were angry and frustrated, none defeated. Even on the meanest streets, there was a feeling of possibilities. The Civil Rights years were still the recent past; progress was, if not guaranteed, at least in the cards. There were things worth believing in and fighting for.

Already that time seemed long lost. When I listened to street kids, I heard paralysis; a dull weight of futility. If I asked how they saw their futures, they looked at me as if I was babbling. What futures?

Crack is often cited as the plague that wrecked everything. In my view, that's a simplification. Crack was indeed a plague, and the cynicism that allowed it to be pumped into the ghettos was tantamount to mass murder. Nor does it much matter, at this date, whether its spread was premeditated or merely depraved indifference. In the ghetto, it's taken for granted that crack was planned, a payback for Civil Rights, and in this case perception is a mutha. Among other legacies, Ronald Reagan deserves to be remembered as the godfather of gangsta rap.

Even so, crack was not the core disease. That was hopelessness. Gangsta spoke to a death of the heart. At least in the beginning, it wasn't a music for African-Americans—the black people who had managed to cross over into the mainstream, with their college degrees and suburban homes, their standardized American speech—but for *niggaz*. The permanently jobless, the semiliterate, the fucked, who grew up without fathers, or with fathers in jail, or, perhaps most pernicious, with fathers stuck in menial jobs, shit work for shit wages. If they tried to study in school, they were called faggots. If they worked, they got minimum wage, if that. And every day they saw drug lords cruise by in luxury cars, bodyguards in tow, fine women all over them. And every day they watched TV—*Lifestyles of the Rich and Famous, Dynasty, Dallas*. They listened to Public Enemy rap about black pride and black strength, yet nothing changed. Then they listened to Ice-T rap about picking up a Glock and squeezing off a few rounds, or dusting off a cop.

Blind rage of impotence: outsiders might call it lazy and self-serving, or argue that gangstas never targeted the true enemy, just their own brothers and sisters, and they were absolutely right, and absolutely irrelevant. The drive to destroy and be destroyed was too intense to hear reason. Live fast, die young, and leave a blingful corpse.

And the misogyny? That came from the same poisoned wells. Frustration, feeling worthless, the fear of being mocked. It would be giving gangsta too much weight to blame it for the wars between black men and women, though it spelled them out in hideous form. That didn't make it less ugly, simply more human. As Soulja Slim's mother, Ms. Linda, says, "Ain't no excuse for most things in this world."

Human misery, human blindness. At root, gangsta rap was a venting, a great incoherent roar born of betrayal and damage. And the fact that many of its practitioners were master storytellers, their narratives lean and riveting, only added to the turmoil. No songwriters in contemporary rock could hold a candle to them. You had to go back to Céline to find the same power to conjure hell that the Notorious B.I.G. possessed. He was a marvel, Biggie Smalls, with a loose-lipped flow that's never been surpassed, and a dazzling writer to boot. In his verses, the mean streets came obscenely, hilariously, unforgettably to life. Even when his lyrics were filthy, they remained spellbinding. On top of which, he sounded so damn good. Hip-hop production had reached full flower and the vilest rhymes were often married to the most seductive beats, so that the best of gangsta rappers made perfect Satans. Even as you squirmed, you fell.

Of course, they denied satanic intent. If challenged, they invariably sought refuge in a litany of cliches: *we're just performers, playing a part; it's only cartoon violence, no one's meant to take it seriously; we're not talking about all women, just the bitches and hos who deserve it; and, anyway, Quentin Tarantino is worse.* It was all arrant bullshit. Even the rappers didn't bother to pretend very hard. Like everyone else, they knew the true name of the game. Get the money.

Nobody expressed gangsta's core paradox—vulnerability in macho clothing—like Tupac Shakur. The son of two Black Panthers, raised by a mother who schooled him in history and politics, he was a poet, an activist, a street hustler, an actor, a thug. He recorded raps like "Brenda's Got a Baby" and "Keep Ya Head Up" that honored women. He served time for sexual assault. He preached self-awareness and the importance of black unity. He fueled kindergarten spats with East Coast rappers, Biggie Smalls in particular, that got people killed. He preached compassion and was in thrall to violence. He was fiercely independent, and he let Suge Knight, the mobster who ran Death Row Records by intimidation, take him over. He was beautiful and vivid with life, and he courted death. Soon enough, he found it.

If gangsta rap had remained ghetto music, it would have had a vogue, spawned some hits, and made a fast mint of money, then slipped back into the underground. Major labels would have gone on pushing the inheritors of MC Hammer and Vanilla Ice, and hip-hop, as a pop phenomenon, would have gone the way of grunge or the New Romantics. What no one foresaw, certainly not me, was gangsta's impact on white suburban teens. Apparently, they didn't want their rap diluted or sugar-coated, after all. On the contrary, the more murderous, the better. Since they risked no physical payback, they could play at gangstas without fear. It was a zip-less fuck.

For record labels, this changed the playing field entirely. Ghetto youths who celebrated killing and the brutalizing of women were degenerates. They bought their records bootleg, contributed nothing to the bottom line. Suburban kids were paid-up consumers. They must be wooed.

The economy of hip-hop, though purporting to be the sound of blackness, had long been driven by the white dollar. And, in gangsta, it hit the richest gold mine yet. The appetite of young American males with money to spend on gratuitous gore was insatiable. Add to that the power of the word *nigga*. At last they'd found something guaranteed to drive the most long-suffering of parents into meltdown. *Nigganigganigga fuckthisfuckthat bitchbitchbitch suckmydick.* Shout it loud.

The trick didn't work for white kids alone. Anyone who drove his father's car—Asian, Hispanic, African-American—could call himself a *nigga* and know, for stone-cold certain, he'd get the response he craved. And the beauty part, for the businessmen who targeted them, was that these new *niggaz* required not only CDs but a complete set of accessories—slang, gestures, accessories, clothing. Better yet, they could afford them.

Hip-hop fashion had come a long way since its DIY roots. New York designers like Isaac Mizrahi had borrowed freely from street styles for years. Now mainstream retailers got involved. Soon every mall in America had two or three outlets aimed at the gangsta nation. Not everyone was welcome in them, though. In the mid-nineties, I spent a week at a suburban mall near Cleveland, observing its rituals. Dillard's was doing a roaring trade in Tommy Hilfiger hoodies and baggy jeans, ghetto style. Every evening groups of black inner-city teens came in and roamed the aisles, while store detectives walked two steps behind, walkie-talkies crackling, until they left and white boys took their place, slapping palms and calling each other dog.

What struck me wasn't merely the reflex racism. In middle America, profiling was business as usual. But the crassness of these white kids playing at blackness, that seemed new. When I, like many others in my generation, had pursued black style in the sixties, it was intended, however naïvely, as a tribute. This was barefaced theft. Casually, as if by divine right, black reality had been kidnapped and turned into a video game.

Call it Niggaworld. A virtual ghetto, where killing and bitch-baiting scored bonus points, and when you were shot, you jumped up unharmed and kept on firing. Because they had so much spending power, the players dictated where rap went and how it was marketed. They neither knew nor cared about hip-hop's past, the aspirations it had once had, or the strength and beauty it might still possess. All that mattered was maximum splatter. When a new rapper appeared on the scene, he was no longer judged by his flow or what he had to say, only by his police sheet, the number of bullets he'd taken, how many notches were on his Glock. Was he a real *nigga,* or fake? That was the one question that mattered.

Who was to say what was real? Sheltered as they were, most fans of gangsta rap didn't have a clue. As the nineties bled toward the millennium, regiments of snarling would-be assassins flooded the market, the vast majority as phony as three-dollar bills. What they lacked in skills they made up in front, and a lot of them got rich off it, which had a paralyzing effect on those with talent. Every rapper, however gifted, now felt pressure to pass the gangsta test. As a result, even the best albums were schizophrenic. If a few tracks took risks and broke fresh ground, there must be some club bangers to meet the bitches-and-hos quota, and of course there must always be slaughter.

The murder of Tupac in 1996, and the fan response to it, exemplified the problem. The ghettos had loved him for everything he was, good and bad, but the malls loved only the bloodshed. After his death, I was walking through a shopping center on Long Island when I heard a group of middle-class teenagers disputing his legacy. The teens were a racial mixture, whites and blacks and one Korean. The last, who argued that Tupac was a genius, was shouted down. Genius? Tupac wasn't no kind of sissy. He was pure gangsta, through and through. Getting butchered proved it. Which explains, in large part, why he was so much more successful in death than he'd been in life. While he lived, he was uncomfortably complex; dead, he became a cartoon. Commercially, he had to be martyred. Niggaworld would accept nothing less.

By 2000, the worship of brain-dead thuggery had hip-hop by the scrotum. The same culture that once had been fearless, that let anyone say anything, was now preprogrammed. From spontaneous combustion, it had turned into murder Muzak. Simply put, rap had lost its nerve. Perhaps as a result, it was selling better than ever. In fact, it had become the ruling force in popular music. The same record labels that had resisted it for so long couldn't get enough these days. On the day I started writing this book, six of the top ten albums on the *Billboard* chart were rap. Hip-hop beats had taken over much of white rock—metal rap, thrash rap, punk rap—and most of the planet. On the streets of Manhattan, I heard Wall Street brokers call each other nigga. No chic event was complete without a scattering of the ghetto fabulous. Glamour dressed in street grime, there was nothing sexier.

Hip-hop had conquered, though not in a fashion anyone could have predicted at its birth. Black musicians and music executives had far more power, both financially and as style-setters, than they'd ever had before. Niggaworld was the hottest, dizziest, most addictive ticket on the market. Get the money? Consider it got.

My own interest was sporadic. The train-wreck fascination I'd felt when gangsta first surfaced had faded. Most of the hip-hop I heard these days was as bombastic and soulless as anything in rock, and I often thought it was time to move on. But music, any music, can only be judged by its best self. On the rare occasions when a new rapper got it right, the adrenaline rush was as fierce as ever. No other music gave me such a charge.

Increasingly, I found my fix in Southern rap. The South had taken a long while to catch on to hip-hop, and it never mastered either New York or West Coast style. Instead, it came up with a curious hybrid: rap rhymes, gospel roots. Many of the lyrics that emerged from Atlanta and Memphis and Houston and, a little later, New Orleans were every bit as raunchy as California gangsta, but they came with deep soul grooves and sanctified harmonies, often carried by live instruments. However vicious their rhymes, Southern rappers sounded human, oddly warm. Outkast, Missy Elliot, Cee-Lo, Devin the Dude—there was the stuff of life in them.

Hip-hop's vitality, the core of its magic, endured, but at enormous cost. By any moral standard, the continued existence of ghettos was obscene. Incredible that America in its imperial splendor could permit such desolation. When I switched on my TV, however, and saw Paris Hilton playing the gangsta ho or Diddy docking his yacht at Saint-Tropez, the perspective shifted. Though Niggaworld was a mighty machine that burned gazillions of dollars each year, it needed constant juicing from below. Without real suffering and slaughter to fuel the fantasy, the whole artifice— mall thugs, high-culture gangbangers, heiress bitches—would fall apart. Human misery, human blindness? Keep 'em coming.

CHOPPA STYLE

Choppa was Take Fo's new signing, just turned nineteen, a glossy would-be gangsta from suburban Marrero on the West Bank, with sleepy, oriental eyes, gold front teeth, the shadow of a mustache. He came into the Sweat Box slouching, loose-limbed, owning the room. An overgrown schoolboy in love with himself. In other words, a star.

That much I knew on sight. D.J. Jubilee seemed to know it, too. The moment the young contender walked in, the old pro deflated. He'd said they would have to carry him out on his shield, but he left of his own accord. "They're missing me on the West Bank," he said.

"Holla at me," said Choppa.

"Fo' sho'," said Jube.

That left Henry the Man and his baby daughter, still asleep on the sofa. Choppa looked at the vacant space where Jubilee had sat. "Don't let me interrupt anything," he said.

He spoke in a swamp-level baritone that sounded as if it belonged to someone much older, and there was a heaviness in his lower jaw and a slight swell around his waist that hinted at a fatter future. For now, his skin gleamed like old gold and his vanity was undented. He believed he was irresistible, so he was.

When I asked how much gold teeth cost, he said $125 a pop. He'd had four done so far but was planning to fill his whole mouth. And what if the world tired of gold teeth someday? He misunderstood, or pretended to. "Ain't about to get tired of Choppa," he told me. "Everyone's wanting me, wanting me all the time, it's like to drive me crazy."

Henry the Man kept chuckling and shaking his head. "Don't be shy," said Henry.

"Shy?"

Choppa was born to bounce. Everything else in his life was just a warm-up. As a kid, he hadn't cared to take orders or pay attention, was always getting suspended from school. To this day, anytime he heard his click was on the streets, throwing bricks up against a wall, he had to be there. "I'm baaad," he said, striking a boxer's pose. However, Earl Mackie had told me he was a middle-class boy, not the project rat he pretended. He came from a close-knit family; his father had a job. At home, Choppa answered to Derwin.

How big a star did he think he could be? "The biggest," he said. A lot of people, females especially, said he looked and moved like Nelly, and he took it as a compliment—Nelly had mad money. "I'ma keep it real and always stay on the humble, but I can't set no limits on Choppa, that wouldn't do me justice."

I asked him to rap and he rattled off a verse to the Triggerman beat, saying he was a West Bank hot boy and made headboards bang all night. Though he hadn't yet released a single and his delivery was clumsy, he had a strong natural instrument, a deep bull-like roar that promised much once he'd knocked off the rough spots. "How's that?" he said.

"Good."

"Only good?" His heavy eyebrows lowered; he pouted. The moment he stopped smiling, he lost his sheen and looked lumpish. Perhaps he was aware of this, because he did a quick half-spin, like a baseball pitcher winding up, and came out of it laughing again. "Verse was tight," he said.

On Saturday night he played a dance in La Place, Louisiana, about an hour's drive from downtown New Orleans. The show was held in the gym of a community fitness center, as impersonal as an airplane hangar. The night was hot and airless, and Choppa himself was rickety, his voice a laryngitic croak. According to his running pardner, DJ Ron, he'd been up in the clubs all the night before. He didn't want to disappoint his fans, else he would have canceled.

Choppa wanted me to be sure I mentioned DJ Ron in my story. "This is my boy, right here," he said. No matter what heights he rose to, he was going to bring DJ Ron with him. Nothing in this world would ever separate them.

A girl in baggy yellow shorts pulled low to show a red thong kept plucking at his sleeve. While her body was lush, the bridge of her nose looked as if it had been flattened with a crowbar. Irritated by the interruption, Choppa turned to blow her off but changed his mind when he saw the swollen wedge of cartilage and purple scar tissue between her eyes, forcing her whole face out of shape. "What's your name?" he asked gently.

"Lateesha."

"Lateesha Pleezetameesha." He put a protective arm around her shoulders and posed for a picture, making sure his faux-gold Take Fo' pendant was properly displayed. Lateesha's girlfriends were staring, wild with envy, and she started to hyperventilate, her giggles turning to gasps. Still gentle, Choppa said he was in a meeting right now. He hoped she enjoyed the show, and maybe he'd catch her later.

I went outdoors for some air. Groups of teenage girls sat around picnic tables, catching any breeze going. Nice suburban girls, they talked about their nails and boys and Destiny's Child and boys. Then Choppa's show began, and they flew into the gym.

Choppa's voice was shot, but he oozed sex. All he could do was croak and twitch. It was enough. "If you like your pussy ate, say Aaahh," he rasped. And all the nice girls went, "Aaahh."

*   *   *

Back home in New York, I listened to Choppa's demo disc. There were five tracks, all entry-level bounce, and he came across fitfully. Though the voice was strong, his rhythm good, he rarely varied his phrasing and his verses, launched with high energy, tended to bog down halfway through.

The obvious stand-out was "Choppa Style," which featured a recurring high-pitched whoop like a rooster crow, jacked from a Beenie Man record. The rest of the number was ordinary, but bounce hits didn't need to be fancy. Given Choppa's stage presence and looks—his *curve appeal,* as DJ Ron put it—that whoop alone might be enough.

I got in touch with Andrew Wickham, my oldest friend in the music business. In the past, he had worked with the Rolling Stones, Joni Mitchell, Van Morrison, and Ah-Ha, and was now a senior A&R man with Warner Bros., based in London. We'd known each other for over forty years and disagreed about almost everything except the very biggest things. Andy was stridently right-wing, a virulent hater, a loyal friend. He loathed rap and everything it stood for, yet he was also a pragmatist. A veteran music man, at risk of obsolescence, could always use a hit. When I told him about Choppa, he simply asked, "Should we sign him?"

A few weeks later, Andy arrived in New York. I had sent him Choppa's demo and he, predictably, hadn't heard a glimmer of talent. In essence, he was taking my word for it, which was both flattering and worrying. We sat in his hotel room and I played him various bounce tracks. He found nothing good in any of them. The next morning, we flew to New Orleans.

We stayed at the Fairmont, a once-classy hotel near Canal Street. Earl Mackie met us direct from his roofing office, still dressed in work jeans and scuffed boots, and we conferred in the Sazerac Bar. For many years, its quasi-Haitian Art Deco murals and air of discreet decadence had made it my favorite watering hole. These days it was loud and trashy, dominated by a flat-screen TV tuned to CNN. Dow Jones quotes crawled along the ticker, and Earl, as if on cue, produced a bound portfolio—Take Fo's business plan, complete with graphs and sales figures and market shares. Choppa, said Earl, was a sound investment. Though still maturing, he had a strong upside.

That night at the studio, the investment showed up an hour late. We sat around the Sweat Box as Earl's cousin Poochie Mackie, Take Fo's chief talent-spotter, tried to keep Andy amused with his versions of the raps Choppa would have performed if he'd been there. They were better than the real thing. Big Man, a one-time gospel singer, provided soulful hooks, and Poochie, who pronounced his name as one word—Pucimachi, like a Florentine Renaissance courtier—turned out to be quite the showman. By the time Choppa finally appeared, yawning, his girl on his arm, the two of them obviously fresh out of bed, his services were scarcely required.

Though only a month had passed since I'd seen him last, he was no longer an eager pup. His name was now known around New Orleans, and Wild Wayne, the biggest DJ on Q93, had started to give him shout-outs. Picayune on a national scale, it was enough to take the edge off his hunger. In place of his former desire to please was a new truculence, a sense of bored entitlement. More gold teeth had been added.

We arranged to meet at noon the next day and break bread. Lunch was at the Daiquiri Hut on Tulane, fifty yards from the studio. Choppa, under pressure from Earl, was only twenty minutes late. He ordered a portion of Buffalo wings with extra sauce and tackled them with an air of long-sufferance. Global stardom was his birthright, not worth sweating, though he was willing to play the game. He even asked Andy Wickham who all else he'd worked with.

Andy, never one for brevity, took eighteen minutes by my watch to reply. Eyes fixed on his manicure, he started at the Rolling Stones and worked painstakingly through the decades. If he had looked up, he'd have seen that Choppa's eyes were closing, globs of red sauce congealing around his chops.

"Where you located?" said Choppa at last.

"I live in London," said Andy.

Choppa looked blank for a moment, then he nodded and showed his new gold teeth. "Europe, right?" he said. "I like Europe. A friend of mine, he took my demo over there, he said they lovin' me in the clubs." He slathered more red sauce on himself. "Europe's good," he concluded.

By the time we left the Daiquiri Hut, Andy had decided to give Choppa a deal, even though he still hadn't heard him perform. Given his distaste for rap, that was pretty much irrelevant. He believed he knew star quality.

I spent the summer at fantasy camp. Andy Wickham had given me the freedom to fashion Choppa's album however I saw fit. While he knew this might yield eccentric results, possibly a fiasco, he was willing to take the risk. So long as I didn't run over budget, and Andy didn't have to spend much time in the studio himself, I had carte blanche.

The proposed budget was $250,000, not bad for a first album in these straitened times. The music business, afflicted by download-ing and bootlegging and its own flab, was in a tailspin. Labels were folding, executives being fired in droves. If you believed the Cas-sandras, which I didn't, the last days were at hand.

In this climate, handing a total novice a quarter-million bucks to play with was either madness or an act of rare munificence. My role, never formally defined, was akin to an old-school A&R man. In addition to overseeing the project as a whole, I would select pro-ducers, provide song ideas, hire guest artists and singers and live musicians as required, and try to keep Choppa's nose to the grind-stone. It was a job description that hip-hop had largely pensioned off. In rap, there were producers, who provided beats and tracks, and executive producers, who in theory ran the show but often did little more than help themselves to a vanity credit and some easy money. Most albums were cobbled together at random, with no overall direction. In New Orleans, only Juvenile's *400 Degrees* had ever aimed at more.

Too green and too euphoric to bother with possible pitfalls, I planned on changing this. Choppa's album would make an organic whole, moving bounce beyond Triggerman and surrounding the raps with all the rhythms of New Orleans past and present—Mardi Gras Indians, marching bands, gospel, jazz, funk—while keeping bounce's excitement and sexual heat.

When I ran my ideas past Earl, he expressed polite approval. It was only later, when my fever abated a little, that I understood why. For a partnership with a major label, he would have embraced an album of bounce-styled Gregorian chants.

Giddy days. Take Fo's deal with Warner Bros. was agreed and passed on to the lawyers, a recording schedule was set up, possible producers and guest artists were reviewed. I took a short vacation in Paris to muster my resolve. On my return, I called Andy Wickham to go over final details. He had, he said, bad news. He and Warner's were parting company. After thirty-plus years, he was out of the music business, and Choppa was out of luck.

I blamed myself. If only I'd kept my yap shut, none of this would have happened. I had blundered in, a loose cannon, raising everyone's hopes in vain. Choppa might be problematic, but, after all, he was nineteen. As for Earl Mackie, I kept picturing him in the Sazerac Bar with his portfolio and his graphs. I couldn't leave him stranded.

More, I wanted to persevere for myself. Though it wasn't something I had planned on, now that the bus had started rolling, I couldn't jump off at the first roadblock. I told Earl we didn't need Warner's; I'd carry on alone. Everything was going to proceed as planned, only without financing or distribution or any sort of sponsorship. Who needed backup? I would mastermind an EP and peddle it to the major labels. "Trust me," I babbled. "It's in the bag."

Earl didn't laugh out loud.

It would be an exaggeration to say he believed in me. In fact, he later confessed, he thought I was crazy. Still, he had been scuffling a long time, he'd had dozens of local hits and was still driving a pickup truck, and he knew that Choppa was his last, best shot at serious loot. If I was nuts, I was a nut who knew a man who'd been at Warner Bros. In any case, mine was the only offer he had.

We agreed to split recording expenses and profits, if any, and I set to work. I dreamed up song ideas, assembled a raft of samples, scribbled guidelines for possible lyrics. Then I rented a converted oyster shack in a mostly black neighborhood, across Gentilly Boulevard from the Fair Grounds racetrack, and headed for New Orleans again. It was late October, the month after 9/11, and the summer's heat was almost gone.

Mary Carson, my then-assistant, worked with me for the first weeks and, in the months and years that followed, Michaela stopped by from time to time to comfort me with apples. For the rest, I was on my own.

What did I think I was doing? Thinking had fuck-all to do with it. I was swept along by a jumble of impulses. Guilt was part of it, hubris another. And something deeper was also at work—the aging male's compulsion to beat against the tide. Other men my age slept with bimbos or bought sports cars or squeezed their loosening guts into tight leather pants; I chased after beats. Most of my contemporaries had started harping on the past, as if totting up their final scores. I wasn't ready to settle.

Money was largely beside the point. I was aware, of course I was, that rap was a billion-dollar business, and a little filthy richness in my life wouldn't hurt, but neither would it complete me. What drove me was the challenge.

Before leaving New York, I swore to myself that I wouldn't front. Whatever befell, I would never make promises I couldn't keep or try to pass myself off as one cool dude. What's more pathetic than a granddad gone wild? Whenever the New Orleans heat allowed, I'd stick to the same uniform I wore elsewhere—hat and jacket and leather shoes, not sneakers—and rise or fall in my own skin.

The oyster shack belonged to an artist, the daughter of an old Creole family whose ancestors had come from France with Sieur de Bienville, the city's founder. She thought of the house as one of her artworks. An aged and skeletal shotgun, unpainted outside, sparsely furnished within, it had no functional lock on the front door and a wooden wedge to bar the back. Dried fronds and palm leaves decorated the walls, the floorboards were bare and the high ceilings stained with damp, and a portrait of Napoleon hung upside down above the fireplace in the front room, his punishment for the Louisiana Purchase. It was a house of spirits, of unexplained shuffles and rattles and creaks. Earl and Henry were convinced it was haunted. No amount of money could pay them to spend a night there, they said, but I loved the place. If there were phantom lodgers, I sensed no malice in them.

My bed was massive and ancient, raised on high like a docked flatboat, with large gaps in the ceiling above it, exposing the cross-beams. At night, small animals scuttled and chattered in the rafters.

Sometime in the second week, I was woken from a fitful doze by a sharp slap on the forehead. I lay in the dark a few seconds and another slap came, this time smack in the mouth. I groped for the light switch, couldn't find it. A third blow just missed me, thwacking against my pillow with a snap like a wet towel. At last I managed to turn on the light. My bed was littered with pecans and pennies and scraps of plaster. The peanut gallery was bombing me.

It was that grim hour before dawn, the time of suicides. I got up and made myself a pot of Community Coffee, black and bitter. The kitchen floorboards were clammy with night sweats, and a woman and man were yelling at each other next door. There was a lot of yelling next door.

When I reviewed my progress to date, it wasn't a pretty picture. Ten days in, and my mission was already in ruins. I was out of my depth, and everyone seemed to know it.

Part of the problem predated my arrival and wasn't directly my fault. To bridge the gap while the deal at Warner's was going through, Earl Mackie had released "Choppa Style" in the New Orleans market and it was a massive local hit. The West Bank hot boy was now a ghetto superstar, escorted everywhere by a posse. He had also acquired a manager, Melvin Foley, a heavyset, smooth-talking don who hung out at Club Platinum, future scene of the shooting that would land C-Murder, Master P's brother, with a life sentence.

Melvin was not in the habit of thinking small. Yes, I could cut some tracks with his protégé and shop them to a major label, but if that label failed to come through with a fat advance, plus a satisfactory guarantee of promotion and marketing, no deal. "This boy here, he's going to be the new king of the South," Melvin told me. "Y'all need to be aware of that fact."

When I went to Henry the Man's house in Pigeon Town to meet with Choppa and lay out my plans, he was busy playing video games on Henry's computer and couldn't be interrupted. I sat in front of a big-ass TV with a blurry picture and watched the colors bleed on *As the World Turns* until he deigned to give me an audience. As soon as I started talking, he yawned, and he went on yawning, stupendously, until I was through. His gold teeth, I noted, were now complete.

I asked where DJ Ron was. "Around," said Choppa, dismissive. His loyalty now was to Earl Mackie and Take Fo'. "Those are my dogs," he said.

Nothing I said impressed him much. He was number one in New Orleans, "Choppa Style" was a smash, so what did he need me for? I tried to argue that there was a wider world beyond city limits, but he wasn't having it. "They love me all over. Baton Rouge, Shreveport, Lafayette," he said. "Everywhere."

Luckily, Earl's horizons were wider. When the Warner's deal collapsed, he'd sent "Choppa Style" to every rap label extant and none of them had even nibbled. He knew Choppa needed polishing: new material, an upgrade in production, more work on his mic technique. At the same time, he had a roofing business to run. Nik Cohn's pipe dreams were not among his priorities, so he fobbed me off on his cousin Poochie.

Like Andy Wickham, I'd been impressed by Poochie's style the night we met him at the Sweat Box. He had charm and gift of gab to spare, and carried himself with a flourish that reminded me of sixties soul groups; he could have passed for a Pip. A roofer, like his cousin, he lived just up the block from the oyster shack and I thought we'd work well together. I was wrong.

Basically, he thought I was a carpetbagger. Take Fo' had labored all these years to catch a break and now I showed up to snatch away the prize and claim it as my own. Every night Poochie sat in the cramped front room under the upside-down portrait of Bonaparte, another snake, and harangued me for hours. His smile never lost its easy charm, so a careless onlooker might think he was kidding, but his eyes were skittery. He said I was working behind his back. Earl Mackie was also working behind his back, and Henry the Man, and even Choppa himself. All of us were conspiring to rob Poochie of his dues.

We kept arguing in circles. I told him some of my song ideas, and he said they were no good. He, meanwhile, had written two numbers that were guaranteed platinum. He sang them to me, and I was forced to admit they sounded hot. The only problem was, he'd lifted them note for note from the new U.N.L.V. *Trend Setters* album. When I pointed this out, he smiled bitterly. "What gives you the right to judge me?" he said.

Came a showdown. I called in Earl and told him I wanted some respect round here, else I'd take my ball and go home. Earl, moon-faced, impassive, made soothing noises and told me to get some rest. I went to bed early and stewed all night. Now this rabble of rodents was strafing my ass.

I took my coffee onto the porch. The front garden, a subtropical jungle, smelled sickly sweet, like a funeral parlor. Across Gentilly Boulevard at the Fair Grounds, the horses in training for the coming season had already started their predawn gallops. The thud of their hooves sounded like a Triggerman beat to me. Another beat came from the house next door. This was owned by a kindly grandmother who ran the neighborhood. Cars came and went all night, dropping off a constant stream of visitors, but early every morning, righteous and looking rested, she was off to Mass. Nobody hassled her, least of all the police. The day I moved into the oyster shack she had told me, if anyone gave me trouble, just say I was staying by her and they'd know to let me alone.

As dawn came up, I took stock. Choppa would not talk to me, Poochie despised me, I had no real financing, no leverage, and—this was the mortal blow—not the first idea of what I was doing. There wasn't one aspect of making a bounce record, it turned out, that I was equipped to handle. As a would-be hit maker, I was beyond laughable. On top of which, I hadn't managed to sleep more than an hour at a stretch since I'd been here and had started to hallucinate. Two nights before, coming home late, I thought I saw biblical tongues of flame dancing on the roof of the Fair Grounds' grandstand and a black priestess, immense in a white robe, singing praises to the fire. No question, I was fucked.

And happy. Not simply content, but joyous; fiercely exulting.

The vanities and credits by which I normally defined myself meant nothing here. Nobody knew or gave a damn what I did in my other life. I was just an old white crazyman, bouncing. Have at it.

Rap is highly formulaic. Almost every track follows the same five-step plan. First, the producer creates a beat; second, the rapper writes verses to this beat, most often three verses of sixteen bars each; third, someone comes up with a hook, the catchy part where the dollars are; fourth, the producer adds breaks and "songs" the track, giving it shape; finally, the rapper goes into the studio and, let us pray, makes magic.

Bounce is especially rigid. Nine times in ten, the rappers are simply handed a backing track and told to start writing. The first time they see the producer is at the studio, if then.

I wanted to shake things up. Why not scramble the batting order? Start with a topic or a chord, a mood, a lyrical idea, even a melody line, and build a track from the ground up? Use bounce as a launchpad, then let imagination run free.

On paper, this wasn't the worst idea; in reality, it was a nonstarter. New Orleans, for all its party trimmings, is deeply conservative. Its bastions are ritual and custom; experiment is never encouraged and rarely tolerated. And bounce is no exception. Any rapper who tries to go beyond "Show me what ya workin' with" risks being branded a turncoat.

I knew this well enough but thought it beside the point. My sights were not set on the New Orleans market. After all, "Choppa Style" had sat atop the local charts for the past five months and sold less than ten thousand copies; it had also been rejected by the major labels. If we wanted more than a hometown hero, it was clear we needed to broaden our focus.

Clear to me, that is. No one else could see my logic. Choppa's own idea was to keep recording "Choppa Style" with different mixes until the majors saw the light. By now he was on his third go-round and saw no reason to move on unless his public started bitching. And his posse, of course, agreed with him; that was their job. Look at "God Bless America," someone pointed out. That female had sung the same number for fifty years straight.

Choppa as rap's Kate Smith? It was a thought, but not a good one. When I asked whether he had any ideas he'd like to work on, Choppa looked at me as though I'd suggested he rap in Sanskrit. If it was ideas I wanted, I would have to provide them myself.

To stand a chance, I must find a receptive producer. Take Fo's production stable was small and contentious. Earl, true to form, paid five hundred dollars a track, less than half the going rate of other labels around town. On the other hand, nobody got shot. The result was constant grumbling but few permanent defections. Almost every producer I met would start our first meeting with a diatribe and end with a declaration of love. Take Fo' was rarely referred to by name. It was always "Earl 'nem."

The best tracks on Take Fo's old albums were the work of Supa Dave. They had an innate musicality, a crispness and flair that lifted them above the pack, and the drums were fire. Now that I'd survived trial by Poochie, Earl called in Dave. Soon he was standing in Henry's living room, a large man, shaped like Yogi Bear, with a massive skull and an expressionless gaze. He radiated an absolute and unshakeable certainty of his infallibility.

Since 9/11, I'd been fooling with ideas for a track called "Stand," a battle cry against evildoers of all stripes. In rap, this meant the enemies of the 'hood—those who preyed on the community and held it up for ransom. I wanted a ghetto anthem, and Choppa had the deep, swagger voice to carry it off.

Among the samples I'd brought with me from New York was a march by Bostich, a Tijuana DJ from the Nortec collective, which matched electronica to traditional brass-band figures and a big bass-drum pattern. It had the martial strut and pomp I was looking for, but needed to be bounced. When I played it for Supa Dave, he placed three salami-like fingers over his heart. With one he tapped out Bostich's beat, with the second Triggerman, with the third a synthesis of the two. After maybe twenty seconds, he signaled that he'd heard enough. I started to expound on my ideas; he cut me short. "I got it," he said dismissively.

Next day he dropped by the oyster shack with a finished track. I had rented a CD player with enormous twin speakers, the stuff of block parties, and these were enthroned in their own room. Supa Dave wasn't eager to hear them. Like Earl and Henry, he sensed the presence of spirits. Murdered slaves were buried under the floorboards, he thought, close to where the speakers now sat. Anyway, he said, he didn't care for big speakers.

Freed of restrictions, Dave had come up with a roiling, pounding piece guaranteed to put the fear of Choppa into any and all malefactors. The emotional climate of the Tijuana original was intact while the music, especially the drums, was pure New Orleans. The only slight weakness was the bass line, which I thought could use a touch more fatness. I called him to offer hallelujahs, but Dave wasn't excited. He already knew how good he was and didn't need me to tell him. Then I mentioned the bass line, and apathy turned to ice. I had overstepped my bounds.

For the moment, all seemed set fair. Not only did I have a killer track to hand, but Earl, impressed and perhaps surprised by how convincingly Dave had met the challenge of a new direction, began to line up other producers. Among them was a newcomer, Playa Will, straight name William Nelson.

Will was Dave's diametric opposite—light-skinned, softly spoken, genteel. He worked as a night manager at a French Quarter hotel and carried himself like an executive on his way up, with courtly manners and a deep voice that owed a little to Barry White. The first time he came to the house, he carried his demo CD in a plastic folder, and his wife of three years, the mother of his two young children, rang him every few minutes to check on how things were going.

The oyster shack didn't bother him. He sat right next to the speakers and chain-smoked Kools and drank Bud Ice, the picture of placid indulgence. When I asked him if he felt a presence, he thought I meant the drains.

Beer and his wife's cooking had given him a premature paunch. With his round cheeks and cropped hair, balding on top, he looked like a well-fed abbot, and this suited his conversation, which was long on morality. His mother and grandmother were both devout Baptists, and Will, though he didn't often make it to church any-more, reflected their teaching. "That wasn't how I was raised" was a favorite phrase. "My soul won't allow me to lie" was another.

More than anyone else I'd dealt with so far, he seemed at ease with me. He was used to whites, he told me later. His mother had made sure he didn't get caught in a ghetto mentality. He'd gone to a mixed school, had white friends all his life. The highest status he could aspire to, he said, was to be known as a gentleman.

I sensed a potential ally. Lord knows I needed one. Until Will came along, I'd tried to ignore my isolation, knowing it came with the turf. Segregation ran so deep in New Orleans that, for many young blacks, there was no question of interaction, never mind friendship. Whites were cops, employers, tourists. The best that could be hoped of them was minimum politeness and a tip. Any white man who went beyond that was likely planning a rip-off.

Every day, if they wanted to eat, blacks must cross into the white world and be humbled. Now, in some small degree, the roles were reversed. Of course, my situation wasn't remotely the same. I had money in the bank, credit cards, connections; above all, I had a plane ticket out. Still, when I walked into a studio or a club, mine was always the only white face. And this was fine by me. It was what I'd wanted, the morning after the Iberville, when 5th Ward Weebie blasted out of that pickup truck and I started walking in his dust. To flip the script, in bounce-speak. Wade out of my depth, with no lifeguard in sight.

No one gave me hard grief. I took a few verbal backhanders, mostly from hangers-on, and there was the odd moment when a pistol in a waistband was left exposed, just to make sure I was paying attention, but I was never threatened, nor did I feel at high risk. No more than anyone else in this slaughterhouse town, that is.

Even so, Will's urbanity was a relief. We had certain things in common, shared a love of Prince and a knowledge of jazz, and spoke approximately the same language. I didn't need to edit my speech or translate it into standard rap usage—Will handled every thought I threw at him, however polysyllabic, and even seemed to relish the change of pace. Though he knew some considered him an Uncle Tom for having any truck with me, his eye was on a bigger prize. He desperately wanted the Choppa project to work. It might prove his ticket out.

He had been too long scuffling, he said. Not yet thirty, he was tired of the bullshit. Back in the day, he'd had a wild streak. Bad things happened around him; he might have gotten shot. Later, when he started producing, he'd worked at South Coast, a local label that had all kinds of talent on tap—beat-makers such as Fess and Don Juan, and a rapper called Bayou Boy who could've gone global but instead went to jail. It had seemed the ideal situation, yet it got pissed away. For what? Foolishness and spite; petty jealousies. Music was all that Will had ever wanted to do, even as a child, but you only got so many shots at your dream. Though his wife was his soul mate and he couldn't picture himself with anyone else, she'd had enough of him making tracks that didn't lead to anything. Every time he started fooling with his keyboard, there was another fight. It couldn't go on.

Every day before he went to work in the Quarter, we'd sit in the sunlit box of my front room, Will chain-smoking and drinking his Bud Ice, while I tried to make some kind of sense. I'd play endless samples—Arabic beats, Algerian rai, bhangra, old New Orleans R&B riffs, pop hooks, a Durutti Column guitar lick, three notes of a Juliette Gréco melody—and try to translate them into bounce, but I didn't play an instrument, had no musical know-how, and so could never demonstrate exactly what I meant.

Will smoked and sipped, and didn't tell me I was full of shit. His own tracks, though musicianly, tended to be over-cautious. He played guitar and piano and had some knowledge of chord structures, not necessarily a bonus in rap. At his best, he had a rare feel for New Orleans street beats; at other times, he sounded mechanical. I kept pushing him to take bigger risks. Will nodded gravely and went away to make more tracks. Next day, when he brought the results, I'd tell him again to take bigger risks, and he would nod gravely and go away to make more tracks. The man had the patience of Job.

Three of his tracks made the final cut. The one I liked best was a Caribbean-flavored beat, complete with steel drums, which we used for a song called "Show the Pearl." The title was mine, and I even sketched a few lyrics. It was a sweet thing, after forty years of wrestling with syntax, to grab up a Sharpie and scribble:

> *Bend it over, catch the wall*
> *Wobble wobble for me.*

DJ Duck was street royalty. He had been working block parties since the early nineties and, with MC Shorty, was responsible for one of the all-time bounce classics, "Where My Ole Lady At?" His speciality was the remix, taking national hits and making them New Orleans. If the studio equipment he used was basic at best, the roughness of the sound fitted his hard-driving, no-prisoners style. I'd especially liked his take on the Ying Yang Twins' "Whistle While You Twerk," and had requested his presence at the Sweat

Box to meet Andy Wickham. Thin to the point of emaciation, he looked, as someone once said of the legendary hustler Titanic Thompson, like the advance man for a famine, with a gentle, tremulous smile and beautiful long hands that kept flexing of their own volition, as if reaching for sounds just beyond his grasp.

Though Duck had recently released a remix album on Take Fo', he hadn't created any original tracks in a while and Earl Mackie was skeptical when I wanted to try him with Choppa. I believed he was worth pursuing and made a pilgrimage to the Ninth Ward, where he still lived with his parents.

The Ninth, sometimes called Psycho Ward, is as deep New Orleans as you can find. Duck's home was hard by the Industrial Canal, a few blocks away from the Desire project, and a heavy whiff of chemical waste hung in the air. The house itself was a brick ranch-style with a small garden, immaculately kept. When I rang his bell, Duck's mother answered. A dignified church lady in a floral dress, she said that Duck was out running an error, but I should come in and wait. We sat in the front room and she served me a soda. The room was a religious shrine. Paintings of black Madonnas and black Jesuses covered the walls, plaster statues of black saints clustered on the floor. "We try to keep it nice," said Mother Duck. That wasn't easy, no. When she and her husband moved in, thirty years ago, the neighborhood was God-fearing. It was like living in a village; people grew their own vegetables; everybody shared. The next-door neighbors, wonderful people, were white. Lots of folks were white back then, it wasn't a problem. Those people had moved away long since. Anyone who was able had moved away. Now there was nothing left, just wickedness and crime, and God was mocked, said Mother Duck, but He would not be mocked forever, no, God always had the last word.

At this point, Duck showed up with his confrere, another Will, and we retired to his studio, a tiny box maybe eight feet square.

Just as his mother's walls were given over to the Lord, every inch of the studio walls was consecrated to twelve-inch vinyl: devil's music at the heart of sanctity.

Duck was in a celebratory mood. He worked days at a sewage plant and had just received a promotion. It felt good to be appreciated, he said. A lot of people had doubted him. He'd proved them wrong.

There was a weightlessness about him, a feeling that he wasn't securely fastened. Ill-equipped for the world's hard slog, he had visions and uncharted deeps. "I haven't bit but one percent of what I have inside me," he said, sitting splay-legged in his box, his body twisting in his chair. His smile, by turn, was shaky, dreaming, luminous. "Just tell me what you need," he said, "I'ma give you magic."

His tracks had a restless, raw-nerve energy that suggested obsession. Every time I listened to them, I pictured a stalker on the prowl. I wanted him to push this further, give it a Psycho Ward edge. At the same time, I didn't wish to limit him. So I gave him a two-bar sample from the Coasters' "Searchin'" and the backbeat from an old King Floyd song, and left the rest to him.

For ten days, I didn't hear from him, then he showed up one night without warning. I expected a beat. Instead, I got a five-minute composition, fully arranged. Magic, Duck had said, and he hadn't lied. The sound quality was lousy, so muffled that some elements came through as ghostly echoes, which only added to the feeling of strangeness. For this music was strange indeed. Cavalry charges of drums were set against spectral stabs of melody and a jaunty little string theme, rising and falling, that ran through the piece like memory: mysterious, nagging, with flashes of pagan joy and an incurable melancholy at heart, much like New Orleans itself.

The next night, I gave the track to Choppa. After a few days, I asked him what he thought. He told me he'd lost it. I gave him the track again. A few days more, and I asked him again what he thought. He told me he'd lost it.

Rappers write their own raps; that is an immutable rule. A rap is a personal journal. To have someone else write it for you is tantamount to admitting you don't have anything to say.

Choppa didn't write his own raps (at any rate, not all of them), but I didn't find out until it was too late. When I heard him in the Sweat Box that first night, I assumed he had picked out the clichés personally. He talked good game about writing and how he liked to drive late at night, working on new ideas. He even carried a notebook at times, and I'm pretty sure I saw words in it.

It was only as the moment to start recording neared and Earl Mackie hooked me up with Bigg Ramp and Lil Tee that I learned the truth. Both were Take Fo' veterans, well respected as rappers and even more so as lyricists, but otherwise polar opposites. Ramp was slow-moving, sleepy-voiced, massively calm; Tee was a rottweiler. Neither had Choppa's curve appeal. Instead, they had talent.

As writers, they were tactful but pragmatic, like bespoke tailors fitting an ill-shaped client. How many verses did I want? What should be the rough content of each? Did I feel it would be a good idea to use another rapper on verse 2, say, for contrast? They made notes and left, and a few days later Choppa's new rap would be ready for its fitting.

Neither Ramp nor Tee seemed troubled by this charade. It was a business matter, nothing more. They were both pushing thirty, past their first flush, and their hopes of more than local success had receded. If they hit the jackpot, well and good; if not, they had bills to pay. Rap was no longer a calling, just a trade.

The next step was to sit down with Choppa and finalize a playlist—which tracks he was willing to record, which went into the

Dumpster. I hadn't talked to him face-to-face for some weeks. He'd blown off a couple of meetings, too busy making money. He could now earn the best part of five thousand bucks from live shows in a weekend, and his faux-gold pendants had been ditched in favor of the real thing. He leased a Porsche and was thinking of buying a house by the lake. Platinum teeth would be next.

Not surprisingly, this affected his desire to toil. Recording was the last thing on his mind, and no one knew how to entice him. Earl had lost control of him. Even Melvin Foley, his manager, was struggling. "He thinks he's all that but he isn't all that," said Melvin. Squads of swooning schoolgirls told a different story.

Supa Dave, meanwhile, had turned two more of my ideas into winners. One was "Brick Jungle," an Ennio Morricone Spaghetti Western track about growing up rough and rugged in the badlands of Marrero. The other was "Jeni Jayne," a stutter-beat paean to strong women that I thought was our banker hit.

Another meeting was set up. This time Choppa showed. Two of his cohorts came along and sat at the long table by the giant speakers, large men sporting heavy gold and working through giant buckets of Popeye's chicken. One of them was named Money.

Choppa yawned, and yawned, and yawned some more. I put up some ideas; he turned them all down. Henry the Man and Playa Will took a turn, and he blanked them too. He wanted to do a song about sneakers. All right, I said, but what about the tracks we already had? Choppa yawned.

Supa Dave was lurking in the doorway over my shoulder, unwilling to step inside the ghost-ridden room. At this juncture, he produced a mini-cassette and handed it to Choppa. It contained a message I'd left on Dave's phone, demonstrating how I thought the hook on "Jeni Jayne" might go—stuttering, trying for a rhythm and, spectacularly, failing. Choppa listened, snickered, and passed the cassette down the table. Greasy fingers dropped their chicken wings; gold teeth flashed, uproarious. Never again would I criticize one of Supa Dave's bass lines.

Afterward, when Choppa and his posse had departed, some thought he'd acted badly. Forget his youth, he needed to learn respect. I wanted to agree, but, in my heart, I knew better. Why should he respect me? Who the fuck was I to come swanning in with my fancy notions and expect him to turn handstands? Whatever his limitations as a rapper, he knew instinctively what worked for him—a song about sneakers, another mix of "Choppa Style." Club bangers had gotten him this far, and he saw no reason to shift. Where I saw a mutual challenge, he saw only an old man's meddling. I was not a record exec, just a half-assed fantasist playing out my senile hungers on his dime. Small wonder he didn't respond. These new tracks were nothing to do with him.

I passed an evil night. By now my sleeplessness was so chronic I'd forgotten what rested felt like. The bags under my eyes were snaked by swollen veins that jumped when I tried to massage them away and my breath was sulfurous. Hep C was having a carnival.

Over Thanksgiving, Choppa gave a series of shows around town and I caught one at a club in New Orleans East, the first time I'd seen him perform since the night in La Place. The hot boy was now the total package. Energy, pacing, stage command, sex—he'd been put on earth to perform. Maybe, after all, everything wasn't doomed.

Earl Mackie, too, saw grounds for hope. If he still thought I was crazy, derangement was no bad thing in the rap game. By the time we started recording, he was prepared to share a financial gamble and move from the Sweat Box to the Ice House, a new studio, part-owned by Juvenile, in a peaceable section of the West Bank. It came at fifty dollars an hour, peanuts by New York standards, serious money in New Orleans.

The Ice House, befitting its name and past function, was air-conditioned paradise. The sound booth alone was bigger than Felton's entire setup, there was a dining area, a rec room with a giant TV, and a private office in back, where Melvin Foley held court one night, regaling me with jail tales and avuncular advice on how to deal with Choppa: tough love. He was a philosopher king, a honeydripper to his diamond-encrusted fingertips; and, in his presence, I felt like a honeydripper too. "There's nothing but winners here," he said, sounding like a carnival barker, and talked of millions and more millions, global domination, platinum out the wazoo, till I wanted nothing more than to stay in that back office, counting fool's gold all night.

Choppa liked to record surrounded by his click—Money, Bigg Ramp, and an assortment of other rappers, Tre-8, Willie Puckett, their friends and managers, and the owner of the Platinum Club and his friends, and baby mamas and their friends. He said he didn't feel comfortable without them, and I saw no point in arguing. He was in a good mood and ready to work, that was what mattered. We cued up the first track, "Dirty Dirty," a club anthem in praise of the South. Playa Will had come up with a basic, powerful beat, Henry the Man provided a hook, and the lyrics, whoever wrote them, had a kindergarten directness. Choppa went into the sound booth and started to lay his first verse. His delivery was hot and urgent, a flat-out bellow from first word to last, well suited to the material. The only trouble was that he kept stopping. Most professional rappers can run through a whole verse, letter-perfect. At worst, they expect to have to redo the odd phrase. One or two takes, three at most, and it's on to the next verse. Choppa worked from word to word.

I couldn't criticize his effort. He stuck it out in that glass box for hours without a word of complaint. The engineer kept cuing the track and Playa Will kept making tactful suggestions and Choppa kept roaring, with full hand movements and body language every time. At the end of three hours, we had completed sixteen bars.

Choppa came out of the booth, a melted man, and we listened to the playback. "What ya think?" he said to the room, and every soul in his click, rappers and managers and baby mamas and friends, said it was tight. That settled that.

There was just enough time to add a hook. It needed a raucous, football-hooligan feel, so everyone piled into the booth, myself included, and we stood shoulder to shoulder, comrades in arms, yelling:

> *If ya ridin' on 20-inch dubs,*
> *If ya baby mama shakin' the club,*
> *If ya show gold teeth when ya talk,*
> *Say what? Ya dirty dirty . . .*

It was only at four in the morning, sleepless in my sweated sheets, with the animal kingdom still rioting above my head, that the reality hit me: I had made a record. More, my voice was on it, riding on 20-inch dubs. Dirty dirty, that was me.

Later, sitting on my porch and watching the horses run, I spotted the grandmother next door coming down her front steps on the way to Mass. We talked about the weather and if betting on horses was crazy. She thought it was, I disagreed. A convoy of three cars pulled up outside her house and she heaved a sigh—no rest for the wicked. "What line of work you pursue?" she asked.

"I'm in the rap game," I said.

Progress remained erratic, when there was any progress at all. By the time the Christmas holidays came and work was suspended for a month, we had completed only two tracks that seemed to me worth shopping. DJ Duck's masterwork had gotten lost so often I'd stopped replacing it, and Supa Dave's tracks were also on hold. That left "Dirty Dirty" and "Touch Ur Toes"—Bounce 101, in Choppa's comfort zone, with no stretching or heavy lifting required.

On their own terms, the tracks showcased him well enough. His raw, charging attack played nicely with Playa Will's street-grimy beats, the hooks were catchy, and there was no shortage of energy. Still, I couldn't see them as national hits. Purely as a bounce artist, Choppa wasn't in the same league as 5th Ward Weebie, and Weebie had never sold outside Louisiana. Something more venturesome was required.

The options were limited. Choppa had only one true subject: the wonder of Choppa. That in itself need not be a problem. Jay-Z rapped almost exclusively about his own greatness and he had done tolerably. The difference, of course, was that Jigga could back up his boasts.

"Dangle more carrots," Earl advised me. If Choppa was given his head on the bounce tracks, maybe he'd feel generous and meet me halfway on the others. And, to give him credit, he tried. When we went back into the studio after New Years', he tackled Supa Dave's tracks, which forced him to work new rhythms and themes, and stayed in the booth so long I feared he'd collapse. "Stand" came to naught, but Bigg Ramp had written three searing verses for "Brick Jungle," and Choppa delivered them with roiling fury, a hellfire preacher testifying in tongues, over a galloping guitar line and the lonesome cry of coyotes. Marrero, in his telling, was a modern-day Tombstone, blood-spattered yet heroic, where hard men rode the concrete range all day, dealing drugs or death, and at night they drank to survival, for the next morning might be their last. You'd never guess that the rapper lived with his parents on a somnolent suburban lane, awash in the scent of jasmine.

Only "Jeni Jayne" proved more than he could stomach. I had sent the rough track to some hip-hop friends in New York and they were unanimous that this was our hit. Even so, Choppa wanted no part of it. He hated the stutter beat, and a song in praise of strong women seemed futile, when he could be praising himself. Besides, he pointed out, Jeni wasn't a black name. What about "Tamisha Shanique"?

I knew I should give in—forcing an artist to do a track he didn't feel ran against all sense and religion—but petty vengeance had taken charge. I'd suffered too many yawns in the face, lost too many skirmishes. So I threatened and cajoled, and Choppa pouted, and we spent weeks in deadlock. Supa Dave was sent for and he presided over a five-hour session that ended with Choppa staging a sit-down strike. Writers and other rappers were added, then subtracted; even Playa Will took a turn as arbitrator. "Dangle more carrots," Earl Mackie kept saying. Nothing worked. What we had here was a failure to communicate.

Too squeamish to do my own bullying, I dreamed up an alter ego to do the dirty work for me: Mort "It's in the Bag" Ziploc. I pictured a leathery survivor from Brill Building days, foul-mouthed, Mob-connected, shirt open to the navel. A gross and hairy man of many gold medallions, Morty was designed to provide the bombast I lacked. As subtle as a chain saw, he ripped into Choppa with all guns blazing. And Choppa, for a wonder, gave in. Maybe he saw that pretending surrender was the only way to get me off his back, or maybe Morty had his number. At any event, he turned submissive. The studio was emptied of his posse, and we whipped through the whole song, intro and hook and two verses, without a break. Choppa was good-humored throughout. When he messed up, he simply said "My bad" and tried again. If it was an act, I was happy to be seduced.

The finished record still didn't work. The beat wasn't right for him. But honor had been satisfied, and the upbeat mood carried over to our next and final session. With the end in sight, Choppa turned on the charm full-bore. He was again the overgrown schoolboy I'd first met at the Sweat Box, prankish and ebullient.

He called me his dog, and we smoked a peace spliff. "When you go in those record labels, you tell them I'm not taking no less than a million," he said, then corrected himself. "Two million." But he was laughing as he said it.

As a parting gift, he gave me a brand-new glossy of himself, signed to "Nik da Trik." After a few more tokes, this morphed into Triksta.

There was rich irony here. In African folklore, the trickster is a central figure, Esu-Elegbara; in voodoo, his name is Papa Legba. And, in black America, he remains the great signifier: the joker, the storyteller, the liar. The one who wears the mask.

Triksta? In my dreams. After that night, neither Choppa nor anyone else ever called me by that name again. Never mind; I hung on to it. It became my code word for my own absurdities, a counterbalance to Mort Ziploc. Every time I started to take myself too solemnly, to fool myself that I really knew what I was doing, I'd take a quick look in the shaving mirror and confront—gray-whiskered, scraggle-necked, *white*—the once and future Triksta, Don of Dons.

Reality didn't kick in again till I was back home in New York, rested and freshly laundered, and I listened to the Choppa tracks on a boom box. Studios are notorious liars; their sound systems are so good that virtually anything sounds like money. Even my block-party speakers were geared to fantasy. My boom box gave it to me straight. And the word was not so hot.

Everything but "Brick Jungle" felt weak. The sonic quality was watery, the beats lacked depth, and Choppa himself kept running short of wind. Clearly, that was my fault. Any rap-meister worth his bling would have spotted the problems and known how to finesse them. Not Triksta. He'd been too busy signifying.

What survived was raw energy. Most likely, it wasn't enough to win Choppa his two million, though it might get him through a few doors. The question was where to start knocking. While there'd been a time when my contacts in the music industry were many and influential, that was in another life. When I burrowed through my old address books, I realized I still knew many powerful people. The only problem was that they were almost all dead.

Through Andy Wickham, I got the name and number of an entertainment lawyer with the splendidly serpentine name of Micheline Levine, who specialized in hip-hop and had represented, among others, Pete Rock, Memphis Bleek, Funkmaster Flash, and A Tribe Called Quest. I sent her Choppa's tracks and she, a little to my surprise, thought they were hot. We arranged to meet for lunch and a tiny, exquisite person appeared—an even less likely rapster, if possible, than myself.

Insubstantial though she looked, Micheline had a determined chin and a no-nonsense manner. She gave me an appraising glance, understood she was dealing with a rube, and took me in hand. If I wanted her to shop the tracks, she said, she'd be willing. Before we went any further, though, I needed to know the facts of life. Rap was a sick and hideous business, and those with the most power were the worst of all. Thieving, lying, conniving—she couldn't think why anyone with options would want to get involved.

Here was the basic deal. A rapper making his first album, without advance fanfare or powerful connections, could expect a budget of about $200,000. Of that, he would receive, typically, ten percent as an advance. The rest went into album expenses—studio time, producer payments, live musicians, mixing, transportation, hotels, whatever. If any cash was left over, the artist either took the lot or, if he was a generous sort, split it with his executive producers. As for royalties, those ranged between ten and fifteen points. Thirteen was usual, with eleven going to the artist, one to the producer of each track, and the last to the executive producers. In other words, provided the album went into profit, I could expect to divide one percent with Take Fo'. Micheline's strong advice was not to put in my order for that private jet right away.

When I relayed the math to Earl Mackie, he was both delighted and appalled. Delighted by the prospect of a budget of two hundred large, since Take Fo' made albums for under ten grand, and appalled at the prospect of giving Choppa the glutton's share of royalties. Surely five percent was enough? Six? Not if I'm your attorney, said Micheline.

The first round of Choppa submissions brought a number of brisk turndowns and a couple of mild flutters. MCA showed interest but didn't follow through. The only serious bite came from Mo Ostin at DreamWorks.

In the music business, anyone who's been around long enough, from Status Quo's roadie to the guy who once swept floors at Sun Records, qualifies as a legend. Mo Ostin is the real thing. He ran Warner Bros. from the 1960s until the mid-nineties, decades in which it dominated the industry, and his résumé started with Errol Garner and wound via Frank Sinatra to Van Morrison, Joni Mitchell, James Taylor, Rod Stewart, the Grateful Dead, and Fleetwood Mac. Some of these were dubious credentials in my book. But Ostin had also signed Prince. That was enough for me.

It was mid-February when I flew to Los Angeles, out of a New York blizzard into California sunlight. For my big meeting at DreamWorks, I sported my standard getup—dark suit, fedora, tie—and an utter idiot I felt, surrounded by T-shirts and ripped shorts. When I said I had an appointment with Mo Ostin, the receptionist regarded me with stony disbelief. "Is this an accountancy matter?" she asked.

The question may have been loaded, for DreamWorks Records was not in good shape. Ostin, to the horror of music-biz veterans, had been forced out of Warner's in a power death-match and

DreamWorks was meant to be his vindication. So far, according to which doomsayer you believed, it was either tens or hundreds of millions in the red.

One of the key problems was the label's lack of success in hip-hop. A major reason for rap's belated popularity with the major labels was that it came cheap. To break a new white pop act cost millions in promotion. Apart from the country star Toby Keith, DreamWorks's most notable success to date was Nelly Furtado. Her single "I'm Like a Bird," and her album *Whoa, Nelly!,* had both gone high on the *Billboard* charts. But launching her had required a solid year of touring radio stations, high-priced videos, relentless hype. To recoup, she'd need at least two more hit albums, and there seemed small hope that these would be forthcoming.

Hip-hop, meanwhile, was a bargain basement. All you really needed were Pro Tools and some hot beats; the hype could be left to live shows and underground rumble. DreamWorks, run by old-school music men, had failed to take advantage. Most of their hip-hop signings—Teddy Riley, Erick Sermon, Q-Tip—were past their glory days. The urban department kept changing leadership and direction. By the time I showed up, DreamWorks was a byword for rap agnosia. Which could be taken either as a roadblock or an opportunity. Triksta (or Morty Ziploc) chose to see the latter. Mo Ostin badly needed a hot boy. And $200,000, by Nelly Furtado standards, was just a sneeze. Surely we could—how do you say?—get into bed together.

Andy Wickham, who worked under Ostin for many years, had spoken of me. As a result, Ostin knew who I was and what I'd written, and he welcomed me into his plush private office as though I were a distinguished visitor, not a two-bit chancer on the hustle. A courtly, rabbinical figure in his mid-seventies, with a white beard and a mother hen's protectiveness, he seemed to have unlimited time to give. We sat through a long, unhurried afternoon while he spoke in autumnal tones of Picasso, Sinatra, Choppa. "I believe everything happens for the best," he said at one point, reviewing DreamWorks' shaky progress. "I trust you will not think me unduly Panglossian."

Did that mean we had a deal? Not exactly. By Ostin's own admission, rap was gibberish to him. He could tell Choppa had something, he said, but what? He must leave that up to his urban department. Unfortunately, the man in charge was out of the office. His father had just died; he was grieving. When was he expected back? Ostin spread his hands in the immemorial shrug of Jewish sufferance. Who can put a season on grief?

I flew back to New York and waited. And waited. Months passed, and still Urban Man did not return. Every so often, I'd call Ostin for an update, but he just sighed. He did suggest flying Choppa to Los Angeles and putting him in a studio with an in-house producer, as Warner's had once done with Prince. The cases didn't strike me as parallel and I passed.

In the end, I decided to go back to New Orleans and try to squeeze one more track out of Choppa—the home run that would end all dithering. I felt I'd learned enough from past mistakes to get it right this time. No more bright ideas, no more preconceptions; the keynote would be teamwork. Choppa himself, with DreamWorks in the wind, sounded eager on the phone. He had taken to calling himself Choppa Chop Chop when he called; once he even rapped to me down the line. This was going to be pure pleasure, I thought, as I hopped on JetBlue.

It was springtime at the oyster shack and the jungle around the front porch was riotous with blossom. A meeting had been set for the afternoon, and I sat dreaming on the steps, idly watching the drug traffic come and go. Though it was less than six months since the first time I'd perched here, I felt like a veteran of long hard campaigns, itching to bore all hearers with my war stories.

The hour of the meeting came and went, and Choppa didn't show. So what else was new? Since I'd recently found another rapper to work with, the hot boy had lost the power to torment me. I rang Melvin Foley and told him I quit. Ten minutes later, Choppa Chop Chop called up, contrite. Could we meet the next day? I gave grudging consent and, when he turned up no more than a half-hour late, unleashed Mort Ziploc, who abused him roundly. His attitude stank. He had some talent, not enough. His gold teeth— and this was the unkindest cut—looked like he'd bought them in a pawnshop.

Choppa took it all like a lamb. He even nodded once or twice, though he never met my eye. "Is this the end of Nik?" he asked, when at last I pulled up for breath.

"What do you think?" I said.

"I think it's the end of Nik."

Later that evening, however, he called again and asked if he could come round. He showed up with Sinista, his new producer, even younger than himself, and the three of us sat under the upside-down Napoleon, discussing politics (Roc-A-Fella, Def Jam South) and art (Ja Rule, Nelly, Petey Pablo). It was the first real conversation Choppa and I had had since our initial meetings, and I could tell it was an effort for him. Still, he was bound and determined to please. An outsize spliff was waiting in his car as reward.

Obviously, the threatened loss of DreamWorks was a motivating factor. Not, I thought, the only one. I was his personal Richard Nixon; he enjoyed having me around to kick. For that, he must first win me back. He played me a couple of tracks he'd done with Sinista. They were, I was happy to hear, abysmal. I told him they needed work, and he said I was right. Did I have any concepts I could lay on him?

I had none, so I played for time. I asked how he was feeling these days. Confused, he said. Everyone wanted different things from him, they had him running in circles. It used to be life was simple. Since he had a hit, it all got too intense.

Fucked up? I said.

No, said Choppa. Just twisted.

I put on a Cuban beat I'd been playing earlier, its spiraling horns suggestive of stress, and started to improvise. First verse, I said, these females keep pushing and pulling on you, they've got you twisted. Second verse, these guys that used to be your boyz have turned into haters since you made it big, they've got you twisted. Last verse, this asshole from New York keeps coming down here, trying to push his concepts on you, he's got you twisted.

"Man," said Choppa, "I wouldn't do you like that."

"Do it," I told him. And put him out the door. Halfway down the steps, he turned back to me and raised his right arm in a curving motion, halfway between a wave and a phantom embrace. "I'ma holla at ya tomorrow, guaranteed," he said.

I never heard from him again.

Urban Man grieved on through spring and early summer, and DreamWorks never did pull the trigger. In the end, Master P stepped in and picked up Choppa for free.

Earl Mackie saw this as a last resort. Percy Miller had lost his magic touch and was seen as a back number. No Limit hadn't changed beats or topics in years. Its skating-rink synths and rote gangsta bragging now sounded almost quaint—survivals of a bygone age, circa 1998—and P still didn't believe in paying people. He had recently cleansed his label of most of its old standbys and reconfigured it as New No Limit. Universal, having made a ton of money off the old model, was bankrolling this second coming. The format boiled down to Same Raps, Different Faces, although, with enough fanfare, who could be sure that lightning wouldn't strike again?

In any any case, Earl didn't have much say. "Those are my

dogs," Choppa had said of Take Fo'. Now they'd gone the way of DJ Ron.

For Choppa, hanging with P was the stuff of fantasy. He got to ride around in stretch limos, party at the mansion in Baton Rouge, and star in a video for yet another remix of "Choppa Style," this one featuring his new boss. With Universal in its corner, it made the countdown on BET's *106 & Park* and lingered there for weeks. The track that had been rejected by every major label and laughed to scorn by the New York playas I'd tested it on was now a certified hit. Choppa's fee for live shows doubled, and doubled again. He was mobbed at malls; his quotes appeared in *Vibe* and *The Source*. The West Bank hot boy had gone national.

There were side benefits for myself. A Choppa album, *Straight from the N.O.*, was released on Take Fo' / New No Limit / Universal, featuring three of the tracks we'd made together. The album as a whole was wretched and "Brick Jungle," in particular, had been remixed almost beyond recognition. Still, *Straight from the N.O.* went to Number 51 on the Hot 200, not exactly a runaway smash, but certainly respectable. In any case, what did I care? My name, correctly spelled, appeared in the credits as a co-producer, and I was registered with ASCAP as a songwriter. When I held the CD and looked at Choppa's handsome face, more jowly now, I experienced the pure euphoria that other authors have told me they feel when they handle their finished books, a joy that had always escaped me. I'd got mine.

This was Choppa's zenith. He never managed a real follow-up to "Choppa Style" and New No Limit soon foundered. After Master P dropped him, he moved on to Roy Jones, the great light-heavyweight boxing champ, who ran a rap label on the side. Then Jones lost his title and most of his mystique, and Choppa's next album was consigned to the back burner. Not that he was going hungry, to judge by his latest pictures. He was still working live shows for good money, had built a new house in the suburbs,

fathered a son and married his baby mama. He talked about starting his own label and called some rappers I knew but didn't follow
up. At twenty-two, he had no need. Though Take Fo' still had him
on contract, he no longer returned Earl Mackie's calls. "That's
Choppa for you," said Earl placidly. "A traitor from the jump."

One day I passed by Aftamath, Lil Tee's barbershop in Pigeon
Town. Tee was now promoting a group of teenage rappers he
wanted me to evaluate. Their leader asked me who I'd worked
with, and I mentioned Choppa. The teen rapper looked unimpressed, but a bystander, somewhat older, lit up.

"Ya boy Choppa!" he said. "I remember his day."

INVISIBLE

Junie Bezel, the Magnolia Pepper Girl, spat game like an uzi. She could ride a club beat and play with it, and she could also go deep. Her voice had a brittle, scorched timbre that conjured up the 'Nolia itself, battered yet defiant. And she could write her ass off.

I met her at the Sweat Box, the same night as my first encounter with Choppa. At the time I had heard only one of her tracks, a battle song called "Hey Lil' Soldier." Her rapping on that was pugnacious, and I expected a gangsta. Instead, a primary school-teacher walked in, slim and fine-boned, with cropped hair; high-waisted, tailored pants; formal lace-up shoes; a freshly ironed white shirt; and virtually no make-up. Her front teeth were her own but she had one gold molar and, next to it, one tooth missing. I thought she was beautiful.

We sat on a sofa in the entry hall; dust rose in clouds every time we moved. Junie spoke so low I had to strain to hear, though this struck me less as shyness than reserve, and answered exactly what I asked her and not a word more. She'd come up in the Magnolia. She had been rapping since she was twelve. She had started at porch contests with Juvenile and Soulja Slim. She held her own. She had always believed she could make it in music. Education was important, too. She studied hard in high school and went to college. Now she taught second grade. She had her own house in Gentilly. She knew the value of money. Fashion was her one big extravagance. She liked nice clothes, especially shoes. She thanked me for praising "Hey Lil' Soldier," but showed no wish to discuss it further.

Was she bored? Mistrustful? Or was there something else? I couldn't be sure, then or ever. There was an inwardness to Junie, a sense of private distance that made me feel I was intruding. We circled each other for a few minutes, then I ran out of questions and she left. When we shook hands goodbye, her fingers barely brushed mine and she walked away, ramrod-straight, with brisk, springy steps, as if freed.

A few weeks later, Earl Mackie sent me her finished album, *That's How Mess Get Started,* produced by Supa Dave. Typical Take Fo', it was a cheerfully sloppy affair, bloated with filler and lame feature spots by other Superstars, yet no amount of padding could disguise Junie's talent. Two tracks, in particular, stood out— "Junie Bezel," her signature song, and "Do the Margarita."

On this evidence, I saw her as a crucial player in the Choppa project. When I mentioned the matter to Earl, however, he looked even blanker than usual. "Junie isn't a team player," he said, so I let the matter drop. As problems with Choppa mounted, however, I kept returning to her, wishing we could tap her heat. In the end, as "Jeni Jayne" dragged on and on, going nowhere, I stamped my little foot and Earl, reluctantly, gave me her number.

Junie came to the oyster shack on a Sunday afternoon after church, in a lashing thunderstorm. The city was awash and everyone else looked like drowned rats, while she was as immaculate as before; weather didn't seem able to touch her. Crisp and starched, she walked in with a business representative, a formidable lady advocate who handled the talking, and the lady's nubile daughter, who nodded out on the sofa. From time to time, her lolling head would come to rest on Junie's shoulder, and Junie, without looking, would swat it away like an errant basketball.

The lady took a dim view of Earl and Henry the Man. They had exploited Junie, she said, just as they'd used many other young people in New Orleans. I said I had no knowledge of this and doubted it was true; the lady wasn't open to discussion. If I wanted Junie's services, they would deal with me and only me, and I'd have to pay up front for the privilege, cash on the barrelhead.

My instinct, when accusations start flying, is to feel guilty myself. Before I quite knew what was happening, I had agreed to pay $600 for a verse, about three times the going rate. Even that, the lady implied, was one step above slave labor.

The rough stuff taken care of, Junie set to work. I told her what "Jeni Jayne" was about and played her Supa Dave's track, and she started to mutter under her breath, trying out different cadences. "Do you have any questions?" I asked.

"No," said Junie, and left.

The night of the session, she took the cash from the envelope I gave her and counted it with care. She had written her verse and it captured Jeni Jayne exactly as I'd pictured her, strutting the block in diamond chains and Gucci frames, an independent woman who's known to maintain, who invests in stocks, donates to children, and renovates buildings: "Breadwinna, headspinna, born to be."

It was the first time any idea of mine had come out close to how I imagined, and even though "Jeni Jayne" didn't work out overall I considered myself paid in full. Junie was a fierce pleasure to work with—strictly business, quick on her feet, not a moment wasted. As ever, she gave the impression there was something or someone she needed to attend to elsewhere. This lent her a steely concentration. She nailed her verse in two takes, her ad-libs in one, and walked out checking her watch, too rushed to shake hands.

Her efficiency shocked me. In New Orleans rap, it is a great rarity for anyone to do exactly what they promise. *Mañana* doesn't cover it: tomorrow never comes. Even at this early stage, I was worn down by the endless delays and excuses, each lamer than the last. Every sad story seemed to start with the same line, *What had happened was . . .*

Reviewing Junie's performance, I felt she was the answer to the question that had started gnawing at me: "Is there life after Choppa?"

Not that I didn't see problems. The market for female rappers these days was highly stereotyped and Junie B didn't fit the prevailing mold. There was a time, in hip-hop's golden age, when women made their own rules. MC Lyte and Queen Latifah, even Salt-N-Pepa—none of them catered to standard male fantasies, and it didn't matter. This was a cruder time. The industry's demand was for bootylicious gangsta babes, nude as the law allowed—Lil' Kim or Foxy Brown or Trina, Da Baddest Bitch. In keeping both her dignity and most of her clothing intact, Eve was a rare exception. Even Da Brat, who started out a tomboy, had undergone extensive bodywork and resurfaced as a siren.

What chance did Junie stand, with her almost curveless figure and tailored pants, her shirts buttoned to the throat? In America, I thought, not much. But Europe was another matter. In Paris, say, the same attributes that held her back at home would seem *très chic*. And euros, after all, spent as well as dollars. Better, in fact.

I talked to Earl Mackie and he wasn't happy. Far from exploiting Junie, he claimed, he had given her his best effort. *That's How Mess Get Started* had simply failed to sell. How could she say he owed her money when all he'd made was zeros? To his mind, it was ingratitude, not to mention gross libel, and she didn't deserve to be helped.

This put me in a bind. Although I had no firsthand knowledge of their battles, Earl had always been straight with me and I valued him, so it was no light matter for me to go against him. At the same time, I couldn't bring myself to let Junie B slip away.

She came to the oyster shack a second time, this time alone, and we discussed the possibilities. With Europe in mind, I thought she should look beyond battle songs and try something more personal. I wanted her to stop following trends and write out of her own life. Junie was noncommittal. She valued her privacy, didn't care for everyone knowing her business. She had a good job she intended to keep and would never do anything that embarrassed her family. If I was going to work for her—for her, mind, not with her—I needed to remember that.

That said, she would consider my ideas. "I'll pray on it," she said, her fingers brushing mine and slipping away, goodbye, and Junie was gone again.

If I had any lingering doubts, this meeting settled them. Everything that drew me to Junie was encompassed: elusiveness, pride, the sense of entitlement. She was twenty-three and didn't have a contract, couldn't sell records in her hometown, wasn't even in demand for live shows, yet compromise never crossed her mind. She was born special and knew it, and she followed her own compass, indifferent to normal social pressures. I don't talk to anyone, she told me. I'm not looking to make friends.

The more I thought about her, the less likely she seemed to succeed, and the less I was able to walk away. I played her tracks to Micheline Levine and others; none offered much hope. She wasn't what sold. She sounded like a headache. Forget it. That was the rational thing, but I'm not a rational being.

The next trip to New Orleans, ostensibly my last round with Choppa, was in fact a fresh start with Junie Bezel. As promised, she had prayed on it, and God had told her to proceed. Every afternoon after school she showed up, always in a rush, and we talked about her life and sifted through ideas. She remained reticent. Nothing was offered unless I asked. Still, I started to build up a picture. Her mother had eight children by various fathers and was now a preacher. Growing up in the Magnolia was not a problem once Junie learned how to handle herself. Though walking through the cut at night was scary sometimes, she had kept walking just the same; what else was there to do? She didn't trust anyone outside her family. No one else understood what went on inside her. Those who thought they knew her didn't. That's why it didn't pay to open up. Any time she did, she was let down. Friends made promises and broke them. Told her they loved her when they were just playing. That wasn't right. She was a good person. She didn't need to be hurt.

As we talked, some possible topics for raps began to emerge—"Kleenex," about rejection; "Invisible," about being taken for granted. I dug up an ancient Eddie Bo funk riff that might be doctored to fit the first, a Rachid Taha bass pattern for the latter. Then I called on Playa Will. Or William Nelson, I should say, for he had decided that *Playa Will* lacked dignity.

I was in Will's debt for his support in the Choppa wars; he'd saved my rear many times. In return, I offered a chance for him to rise above Triggerman and make the music he wanted. Unlike anyone else I'd worked with in rap, he seemed eager to bring me into his personal life. He hadn't known his father, which may have been a factor. At any rate, he confided his problems, frustrations, and dreams; even invited me to his daughter's baptism.

Will and Kristy, his wife, lived in a cramped apartment in his mother-in-law's house. Kristy was a Creole poster child, plump and pampered, extremely light-skinned, with a tiny babydoll voice, and the baptismal party, held in her mother's spacious quarters, was likely the most genteel gathering I have ever attended. A regiment's ration of Chicken in a Box ("more cluck for your buck") was consumed with hushed decorum, every platter held exactly so, at half-arm's length from the body, for fear of spillage. Small talk was conducted in a murmur; the men who watched football on a giant screen never cheered or yelled. A lone dark-skinned man, possibly a genetic throwback, sat apart from everyone else, looking glum.

In the small apartment upstairs, Will made his tracks at the kitchen table while Kristy sat watching soaps on TV and dandling her baby, and their three-year-old son, William, yammered for attention. The atmosphere was often strained, and these tensions showed in the music. Though Will had ample ability, his work always sounded reined in, at half power, as if he didn't quite dare to go for broke.

Part of the problem was his equipment—a keyboard on loan from an associate, tin-pot speakers, no power in his drums, no fatness in the bass. A deeper problem lay in Will himself. He was, to put it crassly, too damn polite. I wanted wildfire and he gave me penny candles.

Could this be fixed? I thought so. When Will, after a few Bud Ices, talked about his turbulent youth and the wild man he said still lurked in him, the smooth surface he usually showed the world fell away. He wore propriety like a ready-made suit, tight in the armpits, murder on the crotch. Underneath, I felt, the Incredible Hulk still lurked, waiting to be unleashed.

The tracks Will provided for "Kleenex" and "Invisible" were a start. Junie liked them, and I told myself all would be well. I was financing the project on my own, with a budget way below shoestring—$150 a track for Will, $60 an hour for studio time, whatever was left over for Junie herself—and it wasn't realistic to expect instant hits. Success, in this context, would be a pair of demos strong enough to play to record labels and circulate in Europe.

Afternoons, while Junie sat hunched on my sofa and wrote to Will's beats, I banished myself to the next room. The tracks played so low they were almost subliminal, and Junie mumbled her lyrics to herself, keeping each line private until she thought it was good to go, so I couldn't make out any words, just the shifting stresses of her flow, like code. Spring was rounding into summer, each day warmer and more languid than the last. Palmetto fronds and morning glory ran riot, car radios blasted the new season's hits, and rappers clustered on the porch next door, swapping rhymes.

Every so often Junie called me in to critique a new verse. It was a process of gradual excavation—half-buried feelings winched up to the surface, often against their will. Though many were painful ("Am I hurt? Am I scared / In my head? 'Nuff said"), the writing was strong and personal, nothing secondhand.

Outside her lyrics, she still didn't tell me much, and her getaways, when each day's work was done, were as brisk and spring-heeled as ever. Even so, a barrier had come down. Sometimes, when I talked about people we knew in common, she would snap her head around and look at me with sudden intentness, her long narrow eyes stretched wide. "You spoke my mind," she'd say. Or, "We're too alike." Mostly she just shook her head and laughed, showing her one gold tooth and the black hole beside it. "Nik," she said, "you play too much."

Will found us a studio in Kenner, out by the airport, where we cut two demos in six hours, and it would have been less if the equipment hadn't kept aborting the backing tracks. Junie sat patiently in the sound booth, perched on a bar stool, her face betraying nothing. When the tracks finally read, she laid her verses in half an hour, almost flawlessly. One line in "Kleenex" and three in "Invisible" needed a second take. She put them to rest as neatly as if she were swatting flies.

The finished demos, predictably, were shy of a home run. That didn't trouble me. They were a dummy run, was all. We had established a connection, Junie and me, and where this would lead us, time would prove.

High summer found me in Paris, getting fatter on Bertillon ice creams. One evening Julia Dorner, my favorite co-conspirator, brought a promoter named Jerome Schmidt to my hotel. A pale and chilly man, exceedingly tall, Schmidt told me he was helping to organize a words-and-music event underwritten by Agnès B., the fashion designer, and would like to include me on the bill. Perhaps I might wish to make a collaboration with a techno DJ. Perhaps, I replied. But why not shoot for the moon? While I did not wish to raise his hopes and then dash them, there was a chance, just a chance, that I could call in a few favors and secure the services of . . . drumroll . . . Junie Bezel.

Schmidt fixed his fishy eye on a point a few inches above my head. We were in Paris, where everyone must know everything, so he couldn't confess ignorance.

It is possible? said Schmidt.

Conceivable, I said.

By the next day, all was arranged. *Junie B for Agnès B.*—it had a ring. There was even a fee; five hundred euros. On the New Orleans rap exchange, that was a month's worth of hustle.

When I called her with the news, Junie's response was low-key. O.K., she said, when I mentioned Paris. O.K., when I said Paris, France, not Paris, Texas. O.K. to the fee, the date, the need for a passport. She had family scattered around America and, unlike some New Orleans rappers, had traveled outside Louisiana, though this would be her first trip abroad. How did she feel about it?

O.K., said Junie B.

Was the nonchalance genuine, or was she too overwhelmed to respond? I wasn't certain. With Junie, I was never certain of anything. The closer our ties, the more her core eluded me. Her e-mails were playful and loving, yet I sensed that could change in a heartbeat and I wouldn't see it coming. She was, deepest down, unknowable.

The Agnès B. show was set for late September. Rather than make Junie fly to Paris alone, I went to New Orleans and collected her. By now we had completed a third track, "Doochie," inspired by the life of Brandon Jones and by a story I'd heard of a boy called Lawrence from the Sixth Ward, who went to a club in the Fourth

Ward. The Fourth and Sixth were friendly, the Fourth and Seventh were not. While Lawrence was in the club, some souljas asked him his ward. Lawrence held up both hands, one with four fingers extended, the other with two. But it was dark, and he was dancing, and the souljas couldn't see that his thumb was down on the hand with the four fingers out. They thought he was saying seven. So they shot him once in the chest, once in the stomach, and once in the head.

"Doochie" was the first time Junie had tackled a topic outside herself, and she'd aced it. There was a narrative power and a tragic vision her previous tracks had barely hinted at. The net result was everything rap fans weren't buying these days—passionate, original, and authentic.

Before we got on the plane, Junie wanted me to meet her older sister, Sabrina, who looked out for her. Though she didn't say so, I guessed this was an evaluation. Sabrina, solidly built, pragmatic, had none of Junie's mercurial jitter. Her gaze, as she weighed the upside-down Napoleon and then myself, was unimpressed, though I must have scraped a passing grade: Paris went ahead as planned.

We left New Orleans as partners. At the airport and on the flight up to New York, we swapped secrets—stories of love and betrayal—and I sketched a rap called "52 Lies (You Told Me)." We were about to conquer the world, no doubt. Then we touched down at JFK and Michaela joined us, and Junie shut off. Whatever was between us, it couldn't stand company.

This was nothing to do with sex. For all manner of reasons, lust could never be an issue. What had bound us was solidarity. It had taken months to build, and it perished in a moment. We sat apart on the plane to France. Junie buried herself in the new issue of *The Source* and never looked up. When I glanced across at her, just before we landed, her face had a rigid, embalmed look.

Once in Paris, we had forty-eight hours to put together a half-hour show. Junie would perform four numbers, I was going to read from the magazine story I'd written on bounce, and Benjamin Diamond had agreed to help with the tracks. Benjamin, compact and intense, had collaborated with Daft Punk and was now a successful singer/composer/producer/DJ in his own right. His involvement was an act of high generosity. We met in his private studio and listened to Will's tracks, which Benjamin planned to run through his laptop and remix. Catastrophe. The hooks—the all-important vocal choruses, recorded in New Orleans—had mysteriously gone missing.

Without hooks there could be no show. Junie shot me one look, a poison dart, and went shopping. All the next day, Michaela trundled her around town, scavenging for the best bargains in souvenir T-shirts, while Benjamin labored to salvage something from the wreck. When we met again, Junie rapped in a whisper, too low for Benjamin to decipher. He'd sat up the whole night before creating a new track for her, and now she refused to let him hear her voice. In the end, she kicked us out of the studio. Banished to an upstairs office, we huddled like schoolboys kicked out of class. Junie's voice, faintly audible through the floor, sounded combative. Even at this remove, it was clear she had stopped whispering and was giving the world a sound ass-whipping.

The words-and-music extravaganza, as one of the organizers called it, was being held at La Cigale (the cicada), a fin de siècle music hall not far from the Place Pigalle. It was a superb location, all red velvet and romantically crumbling stucco, though I was in no mood to appeciate its finer points. On the morning of the performance, we still had no hooks and no battle plan. The only consolation was that the rest of the bill seemed equally hapless. At sound-check time, an ancient American beat poet bumbled soddenly around the stage ranting about codeine-fueled nightmares, and a female performance artist rehearsed a paean to her pussy. Schmidt was also on the bill. His line of racket, as best I could gather, was jazz poetry, and he seemed enthralled by his work. He shook Junie's hand without glancing at her or honoring her with a word. Her name on the poster, I noted, was spelled Junie Bee.

I sat in the stalls and watched a man beat on a trash can while chanting something that sounded like "Zoof Boof Djoof Woof, Zoof Boof Djoof Woooooof." It was a far cry from the Seventh Ward.

Amanda Ghost, a scorched-earth rock singer I knew, had come over from London to see the show. At noon, all other options exhausted, I phoned her and groveled, and Amanda, a trouper, came to our rescue. While she didn't care for rap and, as a card-carrying fashionista, could not bring herself to sing about Doochie living and dying in the ghetto, she was willing to handle the hooks on "Kleenex" and "Invisible," leaving "Doochie" to Benjamin, whose keening tenor had the right gospel flavor for grief.

Gray-haired Derry scribbler in black suit and hat, Magnolia pepper girl, Paris DJ, Notting Hill Prada princess—we made an ill-assorted quartet, nothing if not game. Junie, leaving no detail to chance, had brought her own iron with her from New Orleans and arrived for the show in a shimmering old-gold blouse and cream-colored pants with razor-edge creases. Burrowed within herself, she had barely spoken all afternoon. Though her black mood of yesterday had passed, she had no time for pleasantries. This was her big night.

When we hit the stage, the closing live act of the evening, the audience had already sat through many hours of codeine-fueled nightmares and pussy poems and *Zoof Boof Djoof Wooooof,* and they looked bludgeoned. La Cigale was a big hall, with a capacity of over a thousand, and it was almost full, yet the energy level wouldn't have driven a gerbil wheel.

Our performance was cobbled together with string and a prayer. Brief segments of me reading were sandwiched between Junie rapping over beats from Benjamin's laptop, with Amanda's huge voice letting rip on the choruses. Basically, we made it up as we went along.

The first number was "Junie Bezel," performed to the track I'd cajoled from DJ Duck. Ten seconds in, Benjamin's laptop malfunctioned and Junie was pitched into limbo, rapping with no beat. Her body jolted and stiffened as if electrocuted, and she whirled toward me, mouth wide with panic. Her momentum spun her in a full circle, careening out of control. Or so I thought. Before she came around to face the audience again, she'd mastered herself. She vamped and stalled till the beat kicked in, then ripped through the tightest, most ferocious verse I had ever heard her deliver. When the laptop betrayed her a second time, she hardly broke flow. No mere act of God was going to derail Junie B.

We were about ten minutes in when I felt the first ripple from the crowd. It came to me as a surge, a small electric jolt that buzzed my nerve ends and made me stumble in my reading. I didn't know what to make of it, except that I liked it and wanted more. I finished the passage and Junie took over, and now the surge was stronger. I looked over at Junie, and she seemed to be dancing on air. A power was on us, this ragtag gang of four, and it kept intensifying. By the time we reached the death of Doochie, gunned down in the club, with Junie's voice worn to a strangled croak and Benjamin's gospel cries lifting the murdered boy's soul to a better place, we were transfigured.

That didn't get us paid. When we trooped offstage, Schmidt greeted us with a smile like a canceled check. The show was marvelous, he said. Unfortunately, he had no cash to hand; he would have to send it on later. Of course he never did. Diplomacy failed, and so did abuse. Even Mort Ziploc couldn't manage to turn the trick. He demanded to be told why Junie deserved to be ripped off. Was it because she was black, or a woman, or both? Schmidt answered not a word.

This night in Paris, none of that mattered. Olivier Cohen, Benjamin's father, took us all out to dinner, performers and friends, and we sat outdoors, grouped around a long table on a cobbled Montmartre side street. Junie, in the place of honor, seemed pleased by events, if less than overwhelmed. When people handed her glossy photos to autograph and told her they'd loved the show, she thanked them coolly. "I enjoyed it," she said.

The September night air was warm and clear, and all of Paris lay stretched below us, as far as the Eiffel Tower, under a starlit sky. We drank and feasted, and I felt nothing could better this moment. When the time came to go, I gave Junie a hug, a rare thing between us, and told her I was proud of her. Thank you, she said, and hesitated a beat, and then she asked me if I could give her dollars for her leftover euros when we left the next morning. She'd have no more use for those.

The story should end there: *we'll always have Paris.*

Nothing was ever so good again. The connection between us was lost. In its place was wariness and a festering sense of grievance, never spelled out on either side. Nor did Junie's triumph at La Cigale bring her any closer to a record deal. To stand a chance, she needed new beats and industry-standard production, an upgrade in sonic quality. None of this was easy to come by in New Orleans, which lagged a generation behind other cities in recording techniques, as in so many other respects. Only one studio I knew of, Piety Street, was competitive, and that was far outside my pocket.

When the time came to start recording again, I asked around, and the name that kept surfacing was Wydell Spotsville. According to my sources, he was an underground legend. He not only owned his own studio, he slept in it. Apart from church, music was all Wydell lived for. His sounds, bought off the Internet, were constantly updated, and no producer in town, with the possible exception of Mannie Fresh, Cash Money's hitmaker, was more revered.

Supa Dave himself, not much given to praising the competition, turned humble at the mention of Wydell, who had once been his mentor and remained his inspiration. You need to talk to this man, said Dave. So I called Wydell's home number. The phone rang a long time. At last a woman picked up. "Wydell?" she said. "Wait up." I could hear a TV in the background, and loud voices disputing. Someone had taken a car without permission. Someone else, a girl, had brought home a boy who wasn't welcome. Shrill words were exchanged, dissolving into laughter. Five minutes went by, then the phone was replaced and the line went dead.

I called back. The same ritual was repeated. It took seven attempts and two days before Wydell came to the phone. His voice was gentle and sounded bemused. I wanted to use his tracks? Why hadn't I come to the house? He was going to be in all evening; he'd be waiting for me. So I went to the house. Wydell was out.

The next night I tried again. The Spotsville encampment was way back in Pigeon Town, more commonly called P-Town, in the last block of a long stretch of drug corners and ravaged houses, many of them boarded up, though still inhabited. Watching me approach, a lookout shouted, "White meat."

The house itself was a red-brick bungalow in some need of repair. Shopping carts piled high with empty soda cans filled the front yard, along with rusted auto parts and a single plastic tulip. I entered a room where three young girls were braiding each other's hair, while their babies crawled around in front of a giant TV. Beyond was a room full of older women, grouped around a dining table, playing serious cards. Next came a kitchen, a pot of grease bubbling sleepily on the stove, and three men devouring a ham. Finally, through a Plexiglas door and a plastic curtain, I arrived at the studio—a dark cave containing two sofas and a rocking chair, a mountain of equipment new and old, an electric organ, a sound booth and, half-buried under the clutter, Wydell.

He seemed otherworldly: some subterranean hybrid of panda and troll, circular of face and belly, extremely shy, unfailingly sweet-tempered. Though raised in a combat zone, he hardly seemed battle-hardened. His sleepy eyes blinked constantly, as if unused to light, and he spoke just above a murmur, often in a sheep-like bleat intended as humor, though it felt more like a defense.

None of this meant that Wydell was above earthly gain. On the contrary, he took cartoonish delight in getting paid; actually rubbed his hands together, chortling under his breath, when cash came out. His smile then was beatific.

My plan was to have him redo "Kleenex" and "Doochie" from scratch. Junie went along with this but seemed disengaged. Somewhere between the oyster shack and Paris, we had fallen out of sync, and nothing could set us in rhythm again. Her e-mails no longer spoke of motivation or love, and if she phoned and said she wanted to see me, odds were it was about money. When I asked her what was wrong, she told me nothing was wrong. I didn't believe her.

On studio nights, we'd drive up to P-Town at the appointed hour and sometimes Wydell was home and more often he wasn't. His brother Mike said it wasn't personal; he did everyone the same way. The higher the stakes, the harder he was to pin down. The thing you had to understand about Wydell, according to Mike, was that everyone knew his talent except him. He always thought the worst—*What if I come up empty? What if I let these people down?* Then some errand would come to his mind. "Sometimes he here," said Mike, "but mostly he there."

I learned to show up without warning and bust in as Wydell slept, fully dressed, on the studio couch. Once caught, he would submit with good grace, smile sheepishly, grab a plate of whatever was simmering in the grease pot, and settle at his console, ready for instructions. He didn't have any beats ready-made and never offered suggestions.

Junie didn't offer much either. She seemed to have lost belief and, with it, focus. One session, she had family problems; another, money problems; a third, she didn't feel good. Nights on end, we sat in this cave like crash-test dummies, while Wydell played video games on his computer or shopped online for more equipment, and occasionally, at my prompting, shuffled through his library of sounds. All sense of time and purpose blurred; nights bled into weeks. The two tracks that eventually emerged seemed to happen of their own volition, almost by default. Musically, they were fine. Of life they had not a trace.

In the end, I gave up and turned to Supa Dave, Junie's first producer. He worked out of his living room, in an apartment complex in the East. When I played him the tracks we'd done with Wydell, he shook his massive head in sorrow. What the hell were we thinking? he asked. "Kleenex" and "Doochie" didn't represent the real Junie. What she needed were dance beats, strictly club. This conscious shit, dug out of her life, was a waste of time. Nobody wanted to know.

He knew how to wield a scalpel, Dave. Self-doubt was my weakest point, and he found it unerringly. I already felt I'd messed up Choppa with my half-assed ideas. Now it seemed I had done the same to Junie. A couplet from Meredith's "Modern Love"—*Ah, what a dusty answer gets the soul / When hot for certainties in this our life!*—kept running through my mind. Poetic contemplation was not a good sign in a rap impresario. I threw up my hands and left the field to Supa Dave.

For a time after my abdication, my relations with Junie ran smoother. Some nights, driving to Dave's, she'd take what she called the scenic route, past the body shops and hot-sheet motels along Chef Menteur Highway, and we talked almost as we used to, back when we were accomplices. Once, for no obvious reason, she slowed the car and looked at me hard, as if she'd never seen me before or, perhaps, as if she were seeing me again after a long gap. "You play too much, Nik," she said once more, the same way she had in the past. I still had no idea what she meant.

I knew now I would never get her measure. She was not for me to know; it was as simple and as complicated as that. When we were together, I could sometimes get a partial reading. The moment she left, she was gone absolutely. I tried to picture her other life—friends, family, lovers, school, church. She didn't want me there. At the same time, she was possessive of me. When Michaela was in town or friends visited, or I was involved with other artists, Junie wasn't pleased. When I asked her the reason, she thought a space and said maybe she was selfish or an egotist. At any rate, she was used to my whole attention and didn't care to share.

Supa Dave had been hired to produce three tracks: "Doochie," which Junie still believed in, and two club burners. One was "52 Lies (You Told Me)," born of our trip to Paris, and the other "Headspinnas," a prime slice of braggadocio strutting, partly inspired by "Jeni Jayne." All three sounded to me like potential hits, at least in Dave's living room, and I made the mistake of telling him so. Praise equaled power to him, and power was meant to be exercised. He started canceling sessions and stopped returning calls. Even the smallest suggestions were greeted with a basilisk stare.

My budget was almost exhausted. Deadline day was at hand, and we still hadn't recorded "52 Lies." Junie broke out in a skin rash; then she went down with strep throat. Dave's wedding anniversary meant the loss of another week. Junie had more family problems. The brass band that Dave coached was rehearsing. Junie had car trouble. My flight to New York was booked, and canceled, and booked again. Dave still didn't answer his phone.

When we finally went to work, on the last night possible, Junie was clearly tense. Dave, by contrast, was the picture of good cheer, roistering around the room, his big belly swaying like an over-stuffed hammock. He kept telling Junie what she needed to do, and she kept trying and failing. I was used to her nailing verses on the first take; tonight she could barely nail a line. She stood so close to the mic she seemed to be assaulting it. After each flub, she'd slump for a split second, then jump up and charge again, like a boxer after a flash knockdown.

At last she managed a complete take of "52 Lies," except for one line where she was meant to simulate sex. Her best efforts sounded as if she'd been stung by a gnat. Multiple takes failed to spark greater passion. Dave tried to demonstrate; even I ventured some tentative moans. Nothing worked. In the end, Dave sum-moned his wife, who was sleeping in the back room. She came out in her nightgown, a fine-sized woman, asleep on her feet. Dave told her what was required. "Do that noise you make in bed," he said. His wife uttered a genteel snore. "The other noise," said Dave.

"Other noise?"

"The other noise."

His wife shuffled towards the mic, squared her shoulders, took a breath, and let go an orgasmic howl that must have been heard three blocks away. "That noise?" she said, and went back to bed.

The three completed tracks were the best that Junie had done to date. The trouble she'd had with them didn't show. What came through was incandescence, and the beauty of her rhythm. I carried the masters to New York and elsewhere, expecting great things. The industry's response, however, was lukewarm. Boy George and a few other iconoclasts got the point. The men with the money didn't.

I was learning that success in the hip-hop trade has little to do with talent. Some big sellers can really rap; more can't. Think of MC Hammer, Vanilla Ice, Birdman, Diddy. The keys are producers, catchy hooks, and contacts, and the last is the one that really counts. There are legions of God-gifted rhymers in every American city, and most are driving Rent-a-Wrecks. Bentleys are for the connected.

Junie had magic to spare. What she lacked was a passkey, and I couldn't cut one for her. Her looks were too unusual, her attitude too cloistered. I'm not looking to make friends, she'd told me. But the right friends, in the rap game, were more essential than the right music.

As partners, there was nowhere left for us to go. Though we met from time to time and talked about working on new songs, maybe finding another producer, there was too much bumpy road behind us and, by now, I was too bruised. As with all infatuations, the same traits that had lured me to begin with—Junie's independence, her imperious pride—ended by driving me away. Yet she never ceased to move me. Every time she came bouncing up my front steps, my heart stirred. She might not be easy, but she was superb.

The ending was muffled and wretched. I'd decided to write this book and Junie said she wanted to be in it. As a trailer, I wrote a long article for *The Guardian Weekend,* in which I praised her to the skies. When Junie read it, she told me that while it was a good story, she didn't like my description of her clothes. From now on, she would insisist on vetting anything I wrote about her.

A little later, we met and talked matters through. Junie seemed pacified. She'd been upset, she said; she wasn't upset any more. As a result of my story, Southern Comfort U.K. was interested in booking her for a London showcase and a journalist from *The Face,* then on its last legs, wished to interview her. This was good news, and I was pleased for her. At the same time, I wasn't prepared to get involved in the business arrangements. I still believed in her and always would. Put myself at her command? I thought not.

For the moment, Junie seemed to take this in stride. My impression was that she was secretly relieved, though this may have been a projection to ease my own guilt. We went on talking about music, and family, and people we knew in common; I hadn't seen her so outgoing for months. When she left, we embraced, and she laughed. "Okeydokey," she said, and ran down the steps to her new SUV.

Some days later, she called me early, before school. Her voice was small and tight, and she sounded incensed. She didn't want to go to London, she said, and she refused to be interviewed. I didn't even need to put her in this book.

But there, for once, she was overruled.

DREAMSHIT

One night I came home past my bedtime. It was two in the morning when my ride dropped me off, and I wasn't paying attention. As I stepped onto the front porch and fumbled for my keys, there was a commotion in the shrubbery behind my back and two hooded figures emerged, one small, one large. The smaller held something shiny in his hand, but the porch was unlit and I couldn't see what. Gun seemed a fair assumption.

I took a step back, raising futile hands to cover my chest. My assailant flipped back his hood. "You the man from DreamShit?" he said.

"DreamWorks."

"Whatever."

As my eyes adjusted, I saw that he was about fourteen, with pleading puppy-dog eyes and a tiny silver crucifix at his throat, and the something shiny he held was a CD. "We'll pass by later, hear what you think," he said.

"Right after church," his partner said.

After they left, I switched on every light in the house and sat in the bathroom till my breathing stablized. At least this time it wasn't blackness I'd feared; that was progress of a sort. When I looked at the CD label to see who the artists were, there was only a title, "Ghetto Gurl," inscribed with a Sharpie. They had neglected to write their names. They also neglected to come back after church.

Nonetheless, they marked a milestone. After eighteen months in the rap game, I had finally acquired a status: the Man from Dream-Shit, someone worth targeting with a CD.

I owed my ascension to Mo Ostin. Perhaps feeling sheepish that he'd let Choppa slip, he had agreed to finance a series of demos with other artists. By industry standards, my budget—$25,000, to cover payments to artists and producers, studio costs, musicians, legal fees, as well as my own living expenses—was laughable. Never mind. I'd reached the first rung on the rap ladder: playing with other people's money.

This simple fact changed everything. No longer just another hustler hoping to get lucky, I was an accredited talent spotter, perchance a hit-maker. Overnight, I couldn't walk to the corner store for milk and the morning paper without being waylaid. When I dropped by the Warehouse on amateur-talent night, there was a definite buzz. I was hit on by DJs and producers; plied with so many business cards, glossies, and mistyped bios I could've used a shopping bag. That'll be Mista Triksta, thank you.

The same lacks that had branded me a loser—no car, no front, no bling—now gave me an eccentric's mystique. Wristwatches are key indicators in rap, and the fact that mine was not a gold Rolex but a $49.95 Image (Elvis meets Richard Nixon) caused open derision in the Choppa days. With DreamWorks at my back, a gangsta called Brimstone stopped me on Gentilly Boulevard to ask me where I'd bought it and could he get one for himself?

My first choice for the demos was Junie. The others were Che Muse, of whom more later, and Jahbo, a high-voiced R&B singer who sounded like the young Michael Jackson.

I had met Jahbo at the Ice House during the Choppa sessions. One abysmal night, when progress was particularly slow and crabbed, I slouched off to cool my heels in the rec room, across the hallway from the studio. The Saints were losing again on TV, and I was taking sympathic pleasure in watching them suffer, when a voice I didn't recognize began to sing an acoustic ballad. The voice was filled with a terrible yearning. Keening, it drew me out of my chair and down the hall. A slight, unimposing figure sat on a table, legs dangling. His face was hidden by a hoodie, and his posture was so hunched that I thought he might be crippled. No one in the studio moved or made a sound, and the singer didn't look up. He sang about loving a girl with pretty brown eyes, whose man used her as a punching bag, broke her arm and smashed her face, and why wasn't she with him, who loved her for real?

Though the melody wasn't unique, there was a rawness in this voice that went back to old blues singers. When the song finished, the singer slid off the table and walked away. His face as he passed me looked battered and dazed, as if he, not the girl with brown eyes, had taken the beating.

According to Henry the Man, Jahbo had been around a while. He'd even been signed to No Limit once. That hadn't come to anything, though, and now he was just another R&B singer in a town that had no liking for R&B singers. Unsigned as a solo artist, he kept afloat by singing hooks on bounce records at a hundred dollars a shot. Having heard what he could do, I wanted him to provide the hooks on two of Choppa's tracks—"Touch Ur Toes" and "Show the Pearl"—and his kinetic vocals gave both a boost. While bounce was not his forte, he lent style to anything he touched. He was also receptive. In the studio, he asked my input on almost every line. This was flattering, if unsettling. There was an all-consuming neediness in Jahbo that left him undefended. I'd rarely met anyone so ravenous.

He had a child's face, every emotion clear to read. His trademark look was anxiety, eyes downcast, forehead deeply furrowed, yet every so often, if someone praised him or he was given a track he thought he could use, his eyes lit up with a smile of purest delight: Santa Claus had just come down the chimney.

Nothing ever came easy to him. Even his name was a compromise. He'd wanted to call himself Girbaud, after the clothing line. This might have involved him in legal hassles, however, so he settled for a spelling that conjured up echoes of blackface minstrel shows. It wasn't what he intended, of course. Not much in his life was.

Jahbo never went anywhere without his lyric book. Its front pages were filled with color photos of mansions and luxury cars, meticulously cut out and pasted in. I asked which ones he wanted for himself. "All of them," he said.

One night I ran across him in the House of Blues, at a party in honor of Choppa. The hot boy was at his hottest then, the latest mix of "Choppa Style" all over Q93, and the club was packed to the rafters. Fifteen hundred prime gangstas and bitches in full finery got down, and I wedged myself against a railing, so as not to be swept away. Someone kept whacking the back of my head with an elbow. I turned to protest, but the someone weighed around four hundred pounds and had a "Love & Hate" jail tattoo between his eyes, so I let it ride. When I turned back, Jahbo and three associates stood before me, asking my advice on a new song. Knowing little about contemporary R&B and disliking most of what I heard on the radio, I had no business giving an opinion, but the giant's elbow was pounding the back of my head again, my skull felt like a human anvil, and Jahbo looked at me with such trust. Vanity had a brief tussle with reason and, as ever, vanity won.

Jahbo's support group called themselves Snake Eyez Entertainment. They had white T-shirts, with a pair of dice on the front and SOON TO BE A HOUSEHOLD NAME on the back. I didn't have the heart to tell them what snake eyes meant.

Their spokesman was Rommel "Quiet Man" Walker. Quiet he was, and a class act. Dark-skinned, bald, immaculately turned out, he drove a Frito-Lay truck by day and spent most of his evenings driving Jahbo, who had no transportation of his own. There was a weekly cable-access TV show, and talent night at the Warehouse, and countless errands. This being New Orleans, the futility ratio was astronomical. Still, I never saw Rommel flurried or heard him raise his voice.

His faith in his artist seemed unconditional. They'd met when Jahbo was at a low ebb, recently divorced from the mother of his two children and cut loose from No Limit, and Rommel's role was as much counselor as business manager. It was a full-time job, for Jahbo was a man of constant sorrow. Women troubles, money troubles, acts of God—though the black dog took various forms, it was always on the prowl.

Jahbo lived uptown in his grandmother's house, a run-down clapboard cottage on a broke-back side street, two blocks from the oak-shaded splendor of Fontainebleau Drive. Whenever he left home and turned his face toward those mansions, it was a knife twisted in his gut. *So near, so far away*—it sounded lame, he knew that, yet how else was he supposed to feel? When he thought about his life, he always came back to the same image: "I keep pushing on the door, trying to break it down, and inside is this banquet, all them tables loaded down and groaning with food. I can see it, smell it, I can almost taste it in my mouth. *Hold up, save a plate for me*. That's all I ever wanted, one plate. But no."

He was thirty and knew time was short. Though he talked sometimes about quitting music, how could he? Singing was the only glory he'd known. His mother had him at nineteen, and his parents divorced when he was one. The eldest of four, he grew up a loner—*I never had a mother-son-type relationship*. Still, he had no complaints; his moms did the best she knew how. Main thing was, he never went to jail. His high school, Fortier, was known to be tough, ripped apart by ward wars. While he didn't have a warrior's nature, he could have been sucked in, no doubt, if not for a school concert when he sang "A Temptations Christmas." There'd been yelling and rampaging through the other acts, but the minute Jahbo hit that first note, the hall went deathly quiet. *You could've heard a rat piss on cotton*. After that, nobody bothered him. *There was mad, mad love for me. I came through without a scar or blemish.* Instead of wilding out, he stayed in the school library with the musical set. Six of them formed a group, Just Us, and swore brotherhood forever. If any of them made it, they'd come back for the next in line.

Too busy chasing music, he didn't bother graduating. After dropping out, he went to work as a cook and signed with a small label called Uncut Entertainment—*two jive cats from Chi.* Then Mac, a friend from Fortier, was signed by Master P and, just as he had promised, came back for him. For two years, Jahbo lived large. *Beautiful homes, ridiculous cars.* He sang hooks on some tracks by Mercedes and toured with Mac in a group called the Deadly Apostles, decked out in camouflage gear, an accredited No Limit gangsta with the gold and ice to prove it, though he was never paid, not one cent. *That's how they roll. A lot of bling-bling, no kaching.* Then the wheels had started to come off. Mac was tried and convicted for a murder he didn't commit, and P didn't lift a finger to help. *It started to stink up in there.* So Jahbo cut his losses, went back to work as a cook. Everyone in the restaurant looked at him funny, and what could he tell them? *Music gave me heartbreak and hell. I lost my wife and kids behind it, my best friend's got forty years in jail behind it, still I can't let it go. You can't ignore a gift from God.*

It had been a scuffle ever since. The streets were so full of killing, he didn't care to go out after dark. Mostly he stayed in his room, writing. His grandmother was dying of emphysema, hooked up in an oxygen tent, so no one could visit. Whenever I stopped by to collect him, I had to tap on his window and wait till he emerged, a kid let out to play.

Almost always, he had a new song. He'd run it by me in the car or sitting on the sofa in my front room, and bring me to the verge of tears. Each subject was more tragic than the last. Women betrayed him with his best friend, left without a word, died. No one since Roy Orbison had his heart ripped out more often, or sang pain more achingly. Some days he roused me in the early morning to croon a new song down the phone and his voice then was so naked, the passion so pure that I started to shiver. But his gift was capricious. As often as not, when he took the same song into the studio and tried to pin it down, the magic deserted him. The thought of what was at stake, how he couldn't afford to fail, paralyzed his instincts. At the first mistake, his mouth turned down and his eyes filled with despair.

A more practiced Svengali would have known what buttons to push. I didn't. We kept trying different songs, new producers. We even turned to Wydell. Repeated trips to P-Town eventually caught that elusive soul at home and in tandem with Will Nelson he created a track for a song called "Janelle," about the ghost of a lost love. Feeling that my presence might jinx things, I took a long ride around town. When I returned, Jahbo was crying out the name Janelle in a wail so grief-stricken and haunted it doubled me over. The baby mamas were watching *Judge Judy* in the front room, the pot of grease was simmering turkey necks, Wydell himself had the drowsy smile of a fat cat well fed, and Jahbo kept flying his voice higher and higher, otherworldly . . .

JANELLE . . .

JANEEEEEEEEEEEEEEELLE . . .

But this was just a run-through. When I told Wydell to start recording, there was a fatal delay while he cued the track. By the time Jahbo stepped to the mic, his voice had frayed, and the moment was lost.

What made the frustration worse was that Jahbo believed in me and trusted me to make things right. He brought me new songs almost daily, hoping one would please me. He even took to calling me Bossman, which made me uneasy, if not uneasy enough. Though I knew he didn't intend to pander, the name had connotations that didn't bear thinking about. On the other hand, it was obscenely seductive. "I'm just trying to tickle the Bossman's ear,"

Jahbo said once, and I felt a sharp jolt of pleasure, followed by even sharper guilt. "Nik will do," I told him. The ugly truth was, I liked Bossman fine.

Altogether, I was starting to fancy myself. The man from DreamShit had a swagger that Nik Cohn lacked. No matter that, to Mo Ostin, $25,000 was go-and-play-in-your-sandbox money. In New Orleans, it passed for serious finance and let me play the heavy hitter. I enjoyed discussing the rap hierarchy as if I belonged to it. My conversation was peppered with jargon—*product, units, demographics*—and I referenced radio playlists like a preacher quoting the Bible. When hopefuls brought me CDs to evaluate, I handed down verdicts without a hint of self-doubt. *Popinjay*— "a vain, talkative person, from the Old French for parrot"—is one word that comes to mind.

This was exactly the type of vainglory that Triksta was designed to guard against, but my doppelgänger had taken to cheating. He no longer mocked me in the shaving mirror or blew up my pretensions when my hat got away from my head. I began to nurture the hope that someone, someday, would call me Da Trik for real.

Chasing hard truth through rap, I'd created another fantasy. The oyster shack, the mammoth fuck-off speakers, the meetings, the studios, the night rides through deserted streets—put together, they made one more beautiful lie. I could almost fool myself that the man who had walked into the Iberville was dead and buried. The little giveaways that betrayed me when I'd started to chase behind rap—the tightening in the pit of my gut when faced by a group of unknown souljas, the almost imperceptible edging toward the edge of the sidewalk so I wouldn't be boxed in—were now under control. If strangers jumped out of the bushes late at night and nearly made me piss my pants, I could believe that it was nothing to do with race. And this was not total bullshit. I had come some distance. For now, the squawking of ego drowned out how far I still had left to go.

Rap was a fierce addiction and, like all addicts, I'd become an adept at finding reasons to keep fixing. I was hooked on visions of megahits and the vindication that would come with them, and even more on everyday rituals: the moments when a stranger came through my door and cued his track and rhymed. Good or bad hardly mattered; the act alone sufficed. As the beat kicked in and the rapper's hands carved the air and a new set of street chronicles unfolded—beefs and triumphs and ward histories, tributes to the fallen, vows of vengeance on the living, old marching-band rivalries, hot girls past and present, joyrides and busts, surviving Orleans Parish Prison—I felt all black New Orleans spread out for me like a tapestry, and I wanted this never to end.

Addicts must seek other addicts, so I gravitated toward Lil Tee, whose jones for the game was as obsessive as my own. We'd stayed in touch ever since Earl Mackie touted him as a potential writer for Choppa. He had impressed me then, and my liking grew the better I knew him.

Tee was a bullet-headed man of prodigious force and volubility. Blocky, heavy muscled, his whole being hard-packed and coiled, he went through life like a runaway train. He seemed perpetually on the verge of explosion, though combustibility was just one facet of an unusually complex nature. He was also a giver, and a street-corner philosopher. He managed a P-Town barbershop called Aftamath and ran it like a personal mission hall, dispensing advice, running the dozens, alternately breaking down and building up, so that the atmosphere on any late afternoon was close to riot. One of his favorites was a career crack addict who often slept in the shop and had dreams of singing. While some mocked him, Tee saw deeper. Beneath his habit, the rockhead had wisdom. He was an honest man who had his priorities straight, stayed high yet took care of his daughter, paid for his drugs by doing yard work or shampooing dogs, not by stealing. "That's how a role model does," said Tee. "He handles his business."

The rockhead's speciality was Boy George's "Karma Cha-
meleon," although he had never managed to get the lyrics straight
and "You're my lover, not my rival" came out as "Yuri's dead on
arrival." Tee fed him and helped keep him afloat. He even recorded
his song, complete with Triggerman beat and dog barks in the
background, and God help anyone who laughed.

"I'm not a bitch-ass nigga," Tee liked to say, and he credited this
to his raising. He'd come out of the Twelfth Ward, the product of a
one-night stand, and his mother stood no nonsense. When Tee was
sixteen and she found out he was selling drugs, she put him out on
the street. Most of his classmates in high school got shot or went to
jail, but he liked life too much to lose it and saw no glory in getting
locked up. "Fuck dying. Fuck jail," he told anyone who'd listen. On
the streets, that made him an iconoclast. *I'm an upstream-swimming
muthafucka.* He started cutting hair on porches. Every day, it
seemed like, another customer was killed. That only strengthened
his resolve. *The fact that my daddy didn't want to be by me and my
mama was so coldhearted and every time I turned around a muthafucka died, that's what made me what I am today.* He started rapping with a schoolfriend called Big Al, and they had a local hit,
"Fuck Dat Shit." He wasn't the greatest rapper ever, he knew that,
but he believed he had a destiny. It had taken him six extra years to
graduate high school, and he'd done it; no one had believed he
could own his own shop, and he did. He was twenty-seven, and on
a roll. *I'm going to be a muthafucka to be reckoned with at thirty, you
can take that to the bank. Lil Tee's not out here to play.*

He'd recently signed a group of four teenage rappers and was
schooling them with a stern hand. *Stay in school. Don't let me catch
you fuckin' with cigarettes.* When they came by his house, he
cooked for them and made sure they ate their Wheaties. More,
he tried to show them a wider world. *You have to be the stupidest
muthafucka this side of the equator to just want to rap.* They needed
to learn recording techniques, business smarts, the whole nine

yards. The cemeteries were full of fools who thought ignorance was bliss. The trick to surviving was knowledge. *I don't believe in happiness. Happiness is on Channel 64, the Cartoon Network. I do believe in content. Having what you need.* He had so many people depending on him, the pressure never quit. Still, that was why he'd been put on earth. *I'm a man, and I know how a man acts. Shooting muthafuckas don't make you a man, having boocoo women don't make you a man. A man is about his hustle. Scoot, scoot, scoot. A real man is a gangsta. Has to be. He looks to God, but makes his own rules.*

Tee had no time for depression. When someone was killed, that was an end to it; he couldn't mourn. Life came so cheap in New Orleans. Other places, from what he heard, people didn't get killed unless there was a serious beef. Down here, any little excuse was enough. Five bucks, a funny look, the wrong ward, and pow, pow, pow. It was about hopelessness, he thought. Life took more energy than most people had. *There's a lot of stress to living. But killing? Ain't no big thing.*

We spent long hours talking. Both of us preferred ideas to small talk, so we'd mull the state of rap and the universe at leisure, knowing we shared a wavelength. When I visited him at the barbershop, his clientele, he told me later, was unimpressed. "Why you fuckin' with that white man?" they asked. But Tee thought he could learn from me, and I was damn sure I could learn from him. Though he now lived in suburban New Orleans East, he stayed close to the streets that had made him, and this gave me easy access to heroes and villains who would otherwise have been beyond my reach.

U.N.L.V. (Uptown Niggaz Livin' Violent) were among the greatest of bounce groups. Songs like "Drag 'Em 'n' tha River" and "Yella's Revenge" had been favorites of mine for years. Now, thanks to Tee, the men who'd made those classics sat in my living room, making conversation.

Tek-9 and Lil' Ya were two dark globes, their mouths like solid

gold grilles. Side by side, they put me in mind of a ghetto Tweedle-
dee and Tweedledum, taking turns to speak. Originally, there had
been three in the group, then Yella Boy got shot. They talked about
him calmly, how and why he'd been killed and who had ordered
the hit. They also talked about their new album, admittedly not as
hot as earlier efforts, and the business problems that had dogged
them while they were struggling to record it. Those problems were
now resolved, they said, and they were ready to reconquer the
world.

"Our shit still be tight," said Tek-9.

"Has to be tight," said Lil' Ya.

"The way shit oughta be," said Tek-9.

They answered prying questions with patient courtesy yet
seemed oddly nervous. It was only as they were leaving that I realized why—they'd been auditioning. I, who felt like their groupie,
was in fact the one with power. "Bear us in mind," said their manager, slipping me his business card, and part of me wanted to call
them back, sign them on the spot. The other part knew their moment had almost certainly passed and I could do nothing to restore
it, so I let them shuffle away, pants sagging to their knees, forlorn
mastodons.

This marked another mile. In refusing to rise to the manager's
lure, I ceased to be a fan and thought like an executive. DreamShit
serum was in my veins, and clammy, slithery stuff it was. Smelled
like money.

To Earl Mackie, this meant I was finally getting real. Since
Choppa's defection to No Limit, Take Fo' had been in a downswing.
The royalties Earl and Henry expected from Choppa's album were
never paid, so they'd lost their lead horse for nothing. Meanwhile,
a lawsuit between them and Juvenile over "Back That Azz Up" had
gone against them. The decision was under appeal and a settle-
ment would be reached. For the moment, though, they were looking at a mountain of debts, with precious small hope of turning the

tide. Robbing the poor to feed the rich was, said Earl, an old New Orleans custom.

In a last-ditch attempt to right the ship, Take Fo' was reconfigured. As hip-hop took over mainstream pop, it attracted a younger audience. Infant rappers like Lil' Bow Wow and Master P's son Lil' Romeo had annexed a juicy slice of the market, and Earl and Henry decided to jump on board. The *new* Take Fo', trumpeted in Earl's press releases, tapped a talent pool barely past puberty, including Henry's neice, Lil' Brittnay, who had never rapped before, and Melvin Foley's latest protégé, Baby Boy.

Whatever, let's say, mixed feelings Earl had had about me early on, he was eager to involve me now. However marginal my hookup with DreamWorks, it was, as he freely admitted, more than he himself had managed in ten years' scuffling. So we took a ride to Henry's house and met with Baby Boy, who mumbled and shuffled his feet, making me feel like a school principal. Not that he needed to say much—Melvin took care of the verbiage. A bigger Melvin by at least forty pounds since I'd seen him last, he was in mid-season form. If Choppa was the new king of the South, he told me, Baby Boy was the new prince. As a personal favor, and in recognition of my past efforts, he was prepared to let me have first shot at him, only DreamWorks had better not drag its heels. Unless there was a full quota of zeroes in its offer, plus a megabuck marketing plan, Melvin wasn't interested.

When I heard Baby Boy's tracks, I wasn't interested either. Luckily, Earl had another contender on tap, Stevee, who impressed me more. Not quite fifteen, he came from Little Rock, Arkansas, and was the discovery of Take Fo's latest talent spotter, Terry Wilborn, a mile-a-minute mouth who made Melvin Foley seem shy and retiring. Terry had taken the place of Poochie, who'd been put out to pasture, and Stevee was his prime contender. So far the music was standard-issue bounce, with weak beats and forgettable rapping skills. Stevee's glossies were another matter. He was laughably gorgeous, his skin a satiny café au lait, with long eye-lashes and a come-hither pout—the androgynous allure of all tween idols, from David Cassidy to Mario. A blurry video, shot by his mother, of him opening a show for BTK, then a hot teen-rap act, displayed a born mover, with instinctive stage presence. As for his voice, you couldn't hear a word above the screams of pubescent girls.

When Earl, grumbling at the expense, flew him and his parents in from Little Rock, they proved unlike anyone I'd met in rap before. The father, Steve, was a military man, taciturn and correct. Valencia, the mother, whose beauty Stevee had inherited and who obviously ran the show, was all graciousness; and their son reflected them. Respectful and well-spoken, regally self-possessed, he was a straight-A student, a student-body leader in the making. It seemed absurd to think that he practiced the same trade as Tek-9 and Lil' Ya. There was not a molecule of street in him.

This, I felt, was likely rap's future: professional and middle-class, rebellion made family entertainment. If so, I wouldn't be buying the albums. That didn't mean I had any objection to making one.

Stevee's most obvious lack was material. Nothing he'd recorded could conceivably win him a deal. So I set myself to create a pop/rap song suitable for twelve-year-olds; in other words, racy but not raunchy. The title was "Losin' It," and a sinful pleasure it was to write:

> *I'm losin' it, out of control,*
> *Losin' my mind, my body and soul,*
> *Your body's so warm, ooh girl your smile,*
> *Losin' it, girl, you're drivin' me wild.*

What perverse itch was I scratching here? I had no time to probe. Stevee and his parents were in town for forty-eight hours.

Monday morning was back to school, and we needed a finished song.

Will Nelson came up with a catchy, lightweight track featuring a sly harpsichord figure and a pied-piper pennywhistle melody line, and Jahbo was roped in to handle the hook. Six o'clock on Saturday night, the company gathered in the long room of the oyster shack for a run-through. Jahbo, under no pressure, nailed his chorus first time. Then it was Stevee's turn. And he flew. Ripped through his verses in a blur, dancing as he rapped, with never a stumble or a swallowed word. He was a thing of beauty, a star for this moment, if never again. I looked past him as he danced. His dad sat ramrod straight, smiling gamely, and Valencia was smiling too, though her eyes were also brimming with tears, a mother watching her son take wing and knowing, as he was losing it, she was losing him.

Sunday afternoon at Sound Services, a plush studio in the East, we recorded. Earl showed up an hour late and kept to the background, looking glum. Take Fo's money problems were mounting, and I could feel him counting the dollars. Stevee squandered energy by trying to dance and rap at the same time. The hours were adding up, and nothing usable took shape. Then Valencia, who'd been watching TV in an anteroom, came into the control booth and positioned herself directly in front of her son, looking him hard in the eye and mouthing along with his verses. I couldn't hear if she was rapping out loud; probably not. But she caught the rhythm needed and fed it to Stevee, bar by bar, till at last they fused, in perfect sync.

I won't claim that "Losin' It" was a classic. Removed from the studio, it sounded adequate at best, though it did catch Stevee's freshness and something of his sexiness. For myself, though, the session had offered a revelation. Looking over the engineer's shoulder, I'd felt the first stirrings of—could this be?—aptitude.

Maybe it was DreamShit talking, but at last I had a notion of what I was doing. True, I was still clueless around a mixing board, my musical skills would never be worth a fart, but, if I couldn't create a rap record from scratch, I'd learned how to enhance one. I knew what worked and, more to the point, what didn't. I even had an idea of how to pan gold from dross.

In New Orleans, that made me a rarity. Few here bothered to break a record down to its bones, isolating its strengths, discarding flab. They simply piled into the studio and let rip. Striving for maximum macho, rappers cluttered every song with rote ad-libs and overdubs, and their producers didn't bother to rein them in. The net result was unholy mess. A mess, I now believed, I was equipped to disentangle.

Not for DreamWorks, however. When I turned in my demos, the label took one listen and promptly went out of business. An ocean of red ink, the obituaries said. Myself, I put it down to Triksta.

At one level, this was sorry news. In the music trade, everyone needs a sponsor: a *rabbi,* to use the industry's term. Mo Ostin had been mine, and now he was gone. I was almost back where I'd started. Not entirely, though. I had learned much, and felt ready to put that knowledge to use. My appetite for rap was more insatiable than ever; I could focus on nothing else. If another Choppa fell in my lap, I'd know what to do.

Or would I? Was another Choppa really what I wanted? Even if I found another hot boy and parlayed him into millions, what then? I'd been rich once in my life, and it hadn't suited me one bit. No, any resemblance to Baby Williams was coincidental and would have to stay that way. I had found my true level as a tycoon one day when I was working with Jahbo and he said he knew a teenage producer who had a beat we might use. AD lived with his mother in an old rambling house in the Third Ward, and we drove there in my rented Taurus. The week before, a near-tornado had swept through town and a heavy branch had fallen on the car, staving in one side.

In addition, I had recently feasted, well if not wisely, on a roast-beef po'boy, and most of its juices were splattered over my shirt.

Though the neighborhood as a whole was in sorry shape, AD's street was rigorously maintained, a wide avenue with cars in most of the driveways and recently planted shrubs along the middle ground. We parked and waited. When AD didn't come out of his house, Jahbo began to fret. "I got places to go, awards to win," he said. In the end, he went and knocked on the door.

As it opened, I glimpsed the boy producer in the background, his keyboard almost bigger than himself. The rest of my view was blocked by the square-rigged, stern-faced figure of his mother. Instantly, I knew who kept the street and neighborhood in order. She contemplated Jahbo, with his hip-hop baggies and face of woe. Then she noticed me. "Where you goin' with that white man?" she demanded.

"Whoa!" said Jahbo, ever loyal. "That man's from New York. He's a big-time record executive, bound to make me a star."

The mother looked me up, looked me down. She considered the rental Taurus, its cracked windows and buckled door, and the battlefield of my shirt. I could almost see the thought bubble above her head: "Big-time executive, my ass." Her contempt, however, was too deep for speech. She shut her door with a bang like a judge's gavel, and Jahbo came back to the car. Climbing in, he noted my lobster face and, just this once, he smiled. "Ain't no shame in this game," he said.

Put it on my gravestone.

But not quite yet. Within a month of DreamWorks's demise, I was back in New Orleans, hatching fresh schemes. On my first day in town, I went walking on St. Bernard Avenue. It was a street I loved well, lined with bars and social clubs and barbershops. The day was warm, and porch sitters were out in force. Their voices washed over me, soft and languid. Everyone sounded half-asleep.

At the corner of Villere, I heard a big fine woman mention to her man that he needed to get his mind right, else she just might burn him up. Then she chuckled, deep in her chest, and brushed the sinner's cheek with the back of one great hand, a touch so light it must have felt like a blessing.

If I could rap, this was the city I'd try to sing. Failing that, someone else must sing it for me.

WHAT HAD HAPPENED WAS

Early on in my DreamShit days, Will Nelson said he had a song he wanted to play me. It was outdated, more than five years old, yet he believed it was still valid—a track titled "James Darby (Livin' In Vain)," inspired by a nine-year-old who'd been killed by a stray bullet a few days after writing to President Clinton, pleading with him to stop ghetto violence.

When Will slipped the cassette into his tape deck, we were driving near the St. Bernard project. Will had spent his childhood in the neighborhood and pointed out his old house from the highway; it wasn't fancy, but looked solid. "How I was raised, I never felt trapped," he said.

"James Darby" was a hymn to the trapped. Female voices moaned and wailed in the background, a choir of the bereaved, and the rapper's voice was heavy with grief. While the picture he painted—blighted hopes, wasted lives—wasn't new, his voice was deeply personal. Instead of the chest-pounding soapbox rhetoric that rappers normally used to address injustice, the tone was conversational, a man speaking plain truths.

The rapper's name was Che Muse.

My deal with DreamWorks called for demos from three artists, and so far I had two—Junie and Jahbo. "James Darby" intrigued me, though I wasn't fully convinced. For all its intelligence, there was something disengaged about it, a sense of remove. I felt Che Muse was holding back. Even so, I wanted to meet him.

When Che arrived at the oyster shack, he looked like an anti-rapper. He'd come straight from his day job as a social worker and wore a tie, creased pants, a drip-dry blue shirt. Wide-shouldered and well made, with a round, handsome face that reminded me a little of Fats Domino, he was past thirty and carried himself like a grown man, not a cartoon thug.

Che Muse was his given name: "My mother had politics," he said, explaining his first name. As for Muse, that wasn't uncommon in New Orleans. The city had a long love affair with Ancient Greece. Some of the grimiest ghetto streets were named Euterpe, Melpomene, Terpsichore, Erato. Muses took up almost a full column in the phone book, and Che took pride in the name. His idol and model was Tupac Shakur. If Tupac hadn't needed to hide behind an alias, why would Che Muse?

Most rappers I'd met came at me with a fixed agenda. Depending on their act, they tried to hustle me, or tested me, or kissed my ass. Che didn't have an act. He told me later that Will hadn't given him any information about me in advance, not even my color, so he had walked in with no preconceptions, knowing only that I had some connection to DreamWorks and was scouting for talent. This may have been one reason for his lack of front, but not the main one. There was a self-containment about him. He wasn't about to turn cartwheels for anybody.

The first time we met, I was in New Orleans for just a few days, picking up Junie en route for Paris. Will and Che were working on a track called "Necessito," a sex song by any other name, though Latino, which gave it a patina of class. If the hook was nothing special, the beat was live and, when Che stood up in his tie and crisp shiny shirt to run through his verses, I felt the familiar tremor, more powerful than ever. My doubts began to dissipate. Here was the rapper I'd been waiting for.

What set him apart was his inwardness. Even in a sex song, he reached beyond standard bragging to something risky and conflicted, as real sex is. There was an original mind at work, observant, wry, complicated. As for his rhythm, it was supple and free. Instead of rapping square on the beat, he teased it like a cat with twine. Sometimes he scurried ahead in quick tripled flurries, at other moments he lagged. That was how New Orleans sounded when it talked to itself, on stoops, at bus stops, in take-out lines. Che's was the voice of the city.

Commercially, as usual, I saw drawbacks. Introspection was rarely a ticket to platinum, especially in the Dirty South, where iron-lunged bawlers like Lil Jon and David Banner now ruled the roost. Che was unlikely to be more than a niche artist, and that wasn't what DreamWorks had in mind.

Seeing me hesitate, Che offered to finance a demo himself. Social work didn't bring in much, he said, but he also worked with his father, selling used cars. There was a '99 Buick in good condition, less than ninety thousand miles on the clock, he thought he could move in a day or two. Feeling like Scrooge, I ponied up.

We used a little studio in Metairie, owned by Dave Faulk, a musician and producer who, almost ten years back, had earned local fame for his work with Mystikal. He had the strained, unhealthy look of a studio lifer, too long a stranger to daylight. He was also, I realized with a small jolt, the first white I'd met in New Orleans rap.

Che arrived with accomplices: Tom "Beez" Brown, a dreadlocked rapper with bloodshot eyes and an untamed spirit; and Kiane Davis, big and beautiful, who'd been pulled out of a neighborhood pool hall to sing. Kiane, classically trained, had sung professionally in gospel choirs and a spiritual group, and was currently working with the city opera, but this was the first time she had ever recorded. Tonight was the culmination of many years' striving, and she entered in a state of high excitement. When she found that her chief duty consisted of whispering "pussy bueno," her enthusiasm dulled. Still, she was a trouper. "Just tell me what and when," she said, with a slight rounding of her shoulders, a barely perceptible weariness that spoke louder than a banshee wail.

The studio, up a long flight of stairs in an anonymous apartment block, looked like a converted bedroom, and the sound booth was so cramped that, when Che and Tom and Will crowded around the mic to chant the hook, Kiane had to lean against the door to keep stray limbs from escaping. There was a mood of comradeship, everyone in this thing together and fuckups be damned, that I hadn't felt since the first Take Fo' sessions in the Sweat Box.

Che, it turned out, was a compulsive perfectionist. He couldn't let a line go until he'd worked and reworked it half to death. It wasn't a matter of stumbling, like Choppa, but an obsessive hoarding; he couldn't stand to let anything go. When I asked Tom Beez if this didn't get on his nerves, he laughed. "If you have no mind for patience," said Tom, "you don't need to be around Che."

Listening back to "Necessito" next morning, I heard enough to keep the faith. There was a level of musicianship and craft rare in New Orleans rap, and Che acquitted himself with style. No question, he had the makings. All he needed was to trust himself.

When I started work on the DreamWorks demos, my prime focus was on Junie B and Jahbo, and I left Che largely to Will. They'd been friends for years and shared a love of classic R&B— Stevie Wonder, Frankie Beverly, Marvin Gaye. Che's favorite singer, he told me, was Sade. Though this failed to thrill me, I couldn't argue with the results, or the chemistry between artist and producer. There was a richness of emotion in the tracks Will created for Che he'd barely hinted at before. Raw power was still lacking, so the drum patterns tended to sound like empty packing crates falling down a flight of steps, the bass lines like muttered apologies. Nevertheless, the melodies were strong and sure, even anthemic.

Once under contract, Che kept a certain distance. He was never impolite, merely evasive. Our first day of work, he missed a morning meeting and slept the whole day through, so alarming Will that he went to Che's house and started hammering on the door. "Don't do this to me," Will hollered. Since Che was his recommendation, he considered himself responsible. Worse, he saw his life's dream going down the toilet. When Che resurfaced, however, he didn't exactly grovel. He'd needed rest, he said, and left it at that.

For me, this little bout of AWOL amounted to a mission statement. It let me know, right off the bat, that Che's life did not revolve around DreamWorks, and certainly not around me. Come what may, he would follow his own dictates, move at his own pace. A master of passive resistance, he was unusually self-aware, and there was no scrap of amateur psychology I could throw at him that he hadn't already chewed on long and hard. I asked him once if he refused to commit because he was afraid to fail. "Pretty much," he said without blinking.

It was the same with his past. He was in no hurry to confide, yet never ducked when asked. Many months passed before I patched together the rough outline of his life. When I did, I saw at last why he stood apart from other rappers I knew. Though of New Orleans, he wasn't restricted to it.

His mother was raised in the Calliope, his father two blocks away, and both had gone to Booker T. Washington High, once stately, now a rattrap—a metaphor, said Che, for the whole city. In the 1960s, when they became a couple, they wanted more than New Orleans could offer. Detroit was a magnet in that era, much as Atlanta became in the 1990s, so they moved up north, behind work, to Seven Mile Livernois—a mixed neighborhood, not rich, not poor. Between them, they had five older boys from previous marriages, but Che's only full sibling was a sister, one year younger, and he was used to attention, to being at the center.

Every word off his mother's tongue was political. Black history was drummed into him from his earliest memory. He went to private schools, shielded from grime. His mother called the shots, and his father gave the whippings. "I came up good," said Che. Having older brothers kept him grounded and his best friend was white. He'd go by his friend's house for dinner and be fed shish kebabs; even as a child, he knew there was a world beyond grits. "My mind," he said, "was never cramped for space."

The easeful life ended when he was eleven and his parents split up. Some things happened that he'd never understood fully, things he kept meaning to ask his father about. In any event, he and his sister were sent back to New Orleans to live with their grandmother, while his mother moved to California and his father stayed in Detroit. Then his mother rejoined them, only to get sick and die when Che was fifteen. At the time, he seemed to take her death in stride, didn't grieve consciously. Later, a couple of times in his life when he was in trouble, it felt as if her love had come and intervened for him. People didn't die, he now believed. They took on another form.

After Detroit, New Orleans seemed tribal, a smaller world in every sense, though there were compensations: music, friends, roots. Che went to McDonough 35, a good school but not so snobby you lost touch with the streets, and the streets reached out to him. It sucked you in, this fucked-up town. Even when you hated it, you couldn't walk away. Still, coming from outside gave him a different perspective. People who'd never known anyplace else thought the madness was simply life. Che knew life could be more.

After high school, he went to L.S.U. for a year. Mostly, it was partying and acting the fool, but he met his partner Kel there—Kelwynn Napoleon—and they started rapping. Together they made a bounce record, "I'ma Holla at Ya," and it was a local hit around Baton Rouge. They formed their own record label, Mackadocious Music, and toured all over Louisiana. "What did success mean to me? The girls went from fives to nines and tens. I'm saying, the crème da la crème."

After "I'ma Holla at Ya" had run its course and Kelwynn went back to his studies, Che kept going. He started working with Don Juan, a much respected producer who belonged to the same production collective that had taught Will Nelson the ropes. One album was released and another was in the works, then people started going to jail and everything went to shit. Che's bounce career was over. The time was coming for "Livin' in Vain."

He was in his mid-twenties when he wrote it. "I was getting to the point where I had a problem writing *pop that asshole.*" He had a son from an earlier entanglement and was now in a long-term relationship with Andree, a woman he loved and valued. When she told him she was pregnant with their first child, he felt himself move from a boy to a man and put away childish things. Most of them, anyway. If there were still nights when he got foolish, they were now the exception. "No more dibbling and dabbling," he said. He went back to college and graduated. He started working with his father, who had resettled in New Orleans East and ran a used-car business called Affordable Comforts. And he rapped.

He wrote compulsively, driving out by the lake and parking all night while he worked on rhymes. Like any rapper, he wanted hits and the money that came with them—*got to get that green.* He also had thoughts he needed to spit out or they might short-circuit his brain. Everywhere he went, he carried an old shoebox filled with cassettes and notebooks and scraps of paper. "My whole life is in that shoebox," he told me. Once he fell asleep on my sofa and I walked in to find him with both arms wrapped tightly around his box, hugging it to his breast, father and child.

The irony was, all these years he'd spent writing and dreaming, he had never achieved another hit to equal "I'ma Holla at Ya,"

which he'd thrown off in an hour. Most of his strongest efforts—
"Livin' in Vain," "Innocent Eyes," and my own favorite, "God,
I'm MAD (Misguided African Deity)"—hadn't even been released.
By the time I came along, he'd almost given up hoping. If the
DreamWorks demos didn't work out, he would likely be out of
the game, the shoebox laid to rest.

The stakes were high, then. Maybe that was why Che kept cutting and running. He'd drop by the house a couple of times a week
and talk for a few hours, then vanish. When I asked him if he
was hiding from me, he said it wasn't that, he just needed time to
marinate.

Whenever we did spend time together, we seemed to work well.
He told me about the teenagers he met in his social work, how
their focus had started to shift from party party party to thinking
of the future. The end of welfare meant they couldn't just drift.
The girls all talked about owning a business, most often a beauty
salon, and even the boys were less shiftless. That was the power of
rap, Che thought. There'd been so many songs about absentee
fathers, even gangstas had been shamed. Now, when you saw a
group of young bloods hanging on a street corner, often they had
their infant sons with them.

I remembered "Jack and Diane," the old John Mellencamp song.
In its obsession with ballers and bling, Southern rap had ignored
the everyday scuffle. The easy wisdom was that realism didn't sell,
but I wasn't convinced. Served up as narrative, not a sermon, a
small dose of life just might catch on.

Che agreed, disappeared for ten days, and came back with a
song called "Kevin and Kiana," a little ditty about two ghetto kids,
doing the best they can: "They met up at Club Whispers and it
was oh, so gravy . . ."

I also wanted an anthem for New Orleans. So much of rap was
about celebrating where you came from and what you'd survived.
Here, that usually took the form of talking up your project. Why

not speak for the whole city? Always happy to recycle myself, I suggested "Sweet Sickness" as a title. Che disappeared again.

This time he didn't return. Weeks passed, and he stayed out of sight, embedded in the East. Even Will couldn't lure him out. Che kept missing meetings and Will began to anguish. He tracked Che down to his lair. There was a showdown. "I'm not worried," said Will, the next day. He looked scared to death.

Meantime, Will had made a track unlike anything I'd heard from him before—a huge, swelling wave of sound that suggested both a chorale and an African chant. To my ears, it was a quantum leap, though I was too caught up with Junie and Supa Dave to give it my full attention. I made a few suggestions and left Will and Che to fight it out.

A few weeks later, I was with a friend in Liuzza's, my neighborhood clubhouse, medicating my nerves with a bowl of premium gumbo, when Che marched in and handed me a CD. My friend's van, complete with power speakers, was parked across the street, so I left Che at the bar and went off to hear what he'd wrought. After a few seconds, I felt the hair start to rise on the back of my neck.

The song was called "Bayuka." Over Will's slow, liturgical track and a variation on the *Come with me* riff from Tupac's "Hail Mary," Che rapped about spiritual possession. "Something's burnin' in me, and it's hard to keep in me / The soul of a slave named Bayuka lives in me," he began. Bayuka never slept, he kept running around Che's subliminal, stump-dancing to the beat, screaming at him to rise. In the background, meanwhile, a roll call of dead black heroes from Nat Turner and Marcus Garvey to Malcolm X and Bob Marley tolled. Then Kiane entered with the lush, rhapsodic hook. Then Che again, sounding as if Bayuka was ripping at his throat. There was a quasi-classical piano interlude, a choir, a burying-ground bass drum. Total overkill. And I loved it. Of all the tracks I'd been involved with, none owed so little to my direct input, and none came so close to the music in my head. If there was a message there, I was not ready to receive it yet.

Daylight brought few second thoughts. While the sound still lacked fatness and parts of Che's rap needed doing over, the basis was solid, of that I was sure. Besides, Che and Will were already at work on another track, "The Prophet," about rap's power to inflame and heal, that shaped up even stronger. By now, my work with Junie was over, and I could be fully invested. We recorded at Sound Services, the same studio I'd used with Stevee, and the sessions, at least by Che's standards, went quickly. Even he seemed to feel he'd hit a winning streak and was willing to push ahead.

In the end, all four tracks were completed on schedule, with almost ten minutes to spare. When I flew north with the results, I was confident we'd done good work, even if the chances of a deal were no better than fifty-fifty. In terms of mainstream rap, we had wandered far to left field. Che was not a pretty boy, bragging about his dick; Will's soundscapes weren't remotely crunk. In any case, the issue was academic. DreamWorks went belly-up, and the tracks reverted to us. I played them to my contacts in New York and Europe, and the response was good, not great. Almost everyone felt Che had potential. No one would back him with anything more solid than vague promises.

Common sense said that I was through. Without the magic cloak of DreamShit, I had no power, no possible reason to think I might yet prevail. Time to bow out gracefully and let Triksta rest in peace. That wasn't possible, though; rap fever was in me too deep. Whatever it took, I must try again.

My only recourse, having bet on us once and lost, was to double up. I formed my own record label, RoadBurns, and signed Che to it. Then I took the advance for this book and wagered it on his back. I bought our own Pro Tools, a serviceable mic, and industry-standard speakers, and rented a house big enough to encompass a studio. Rather than scratch out another demo, this time we were going to create a full-scale album, and not just any album—an attempt to capture the whole soul of New Orleans, nothing less than the sweet sickness in rap.

The house on Solomon Street was frail. Apart from its sagging foundations and buckled walls, the windows were so old and caked with grime that the glass cracked the moment I tried to clean it. Rather then stare at the blackened shards, I chose to cover them with a job lot of old curtains from Thrift City and live in permanent dimness.

It was early November, two years, almost to the day, since I'd started working with Choppa. Already I'd come to town for a few days in August, braving the swelter and swamp stench to do some advance planning. Che and I had hunkered in my hotel room, air-conditioning set to the max, while he reeled off one song idea after another, each more imaginative than the last. The idea of a rap portrait of New Orleans, unfolding like a movie, seemed to enthuse him, and he was fully committed to Will. When I asked whether he didn't think a whole album might call for more than a single producer, he seemed adamant. There were these two dudes in Birmingham, Alabama, James Belville and Big Bird, who had a top-flight studio and could be a resource when it came time for mixing. But Will was his producer, case closed.

As for Will, he was positively giddy. The three of us met at his apartment, with his son rampaging at our backs and his baby daughter crawling at our feet, her eyes already glued to the rap videos on BET, and he waxed evangelical. We were going to change the world.

That was August. In November, nothing sat right. From the moment I arrived in Solomon Street to start work, Che was at odds with himself and the world. Showing up hours late for our first meeting, he shuffled up the front steps as though his ankles were shackled. The shoebox was gone, replaced by a black satchel that he carried slung across his shoulder like a sack of woe, almost too heavy to haul.

It was only ten weeks since I'd seen him last, yet he seemed ten years older. Mouth, belly, posture—everything sagged. When he sat in the overstuffed armchair that my friend Nan had found at a garage sale, it swallowed him. He looked, in short, like a man who'd been granted his wish.

His former evasiveness was now headlong flight. The main function of my days was to sit waiting on the porch, watching squirrels chasing around the live oak and calling Che on his cell phone, on the hour every hour, to ask where he was and why he still wasn't here. It took us a week to buy the soundproof foam for the recording booth and another week to tack it in place. I had witnessed livelier comas.

Nothing I said or did was any use. Every few days I'd corner him and try to thrash out what was wrong, and it was like Jet Skiing through quicksand. He wasn't comfortable with the new equipment, or he didn't respond to Will's beats, or he thought the three of us should go to Birmingham and work with James and Big Bird. His contract as a social worker had run out, the holiday season was coming up, and he had to chase behind a dollar. Every time we spoke, there seemed to be a new glitch. I'd thought Junie, in our days with Wydell, had a rich stock of excuses; Che's seemed inexhaustible. His eldest son had a basketball game. There was a car auction he couldn't afford to miss. He'd overslept. The mic was sub-par. No, the mic was O.K., but the soundproofing wasn't right. No, the soundproofing was fine; the problem was the beats. His son had another basketball game. His Walkman was lost. His family needed him home. He'd overslept again.

Winter came in early and mean, and the house was unheated. Huddled over storage heaters, I lived in thermal underwear, under blankets. Soulja Slim was murdered, the funeral came and went, and still we hadn't started real work. Will's marriage had broken up and he was living with his mother, seeking comfort in the clubs most nights and hungover most days. When he shut himself in the back room where we'd set up the studio, the sounds that emerged sounded as if they were made on a child's first beat box. Pro Tools, it appeared, was not the magic cure-all we had envisioned. The same sonic gurus who had promised me that it held the answer to our every problem now said yes, this was true, but it took two years to master. The computer kept aborting; we didn't know how to harness its resources or access most of its programs, and our fumblings made things worse. Celeste, the engineer at Sound Services, was enrolled as a part-time angel of mercy. She'd come by and punch some buttons. For a day, sometimes two, all would be well. Then the gremlins crept back.

Nothing was as I had imagined. Back in August, I'd pictured the studio as an open house, where Che and Will could pass through at any hour of day or night and the creative juices would never run dry. The Three Musketeers had been invoked. Now Will was hauling bags as a doorman at a downtown hotel, putting in double shifts until he could afford his own apartment, Che rarely picked up his phone, and when we did contrive to meet and dabble with work, the results were embarrassing. I kept revisiting "Sweet Sickness" and "Bayuka" and "The Prophet," wondering if I had dreamed them. No, they still sounded strong. Rough, unfinished, clunky, overstuffed—you could blow any number of holes in them, yet they had flavor and passion, and they took big risks. Then I'd put on our latest efforts. They sounded scared to breathe.

All thought of a cohesive album, New Orleans in rap, was abandoned. The new target was simply some tracks with a pulse, and even that seemed beyond us. Instead of daring a masterwork, we aimed low, and missed.

Only one night offered hope, and that was an accident. We were hunkered in the studio, sifting through discarded ideas and bitching at each other. Che kept harping on Birmingham, which had become a holy city in his mind; Will didn't want to hear it. They bickered and sulked, and Will, more in frustration than hope, started messing with his drum machine. Suddenly, he found a beat. A simple bounce pattern over a heavy bass drum that conjured up marching bands. Musically, it was nothing fancy, but it had the heat we'd been missing, and Che began to chant over it, *she wants some, oh she shakes some, oh she wants some.* As the beat gathered strength, he started freestyling, mumbling broken phrases, nonsense rhymes. All strain and age went from his face, and he looked exultant. *She shakes some, oh she wants some*—there wasn't a brain cell to it, and it felt so fucking good, all three of us burst out laughing.

The moment passed, and we could never quite recapture it. By the time Che was ready to record, that mindless joy had evaporated and he sounded careworn again. Though "She Wants Some" might well be a hit, we had mislaid its access code.

Too much thought, not enough anger. Great rap, almost always, was born of rage. The world had its foot on your throat, and hip-hop was your howl of defiance. The feeling of being attacked didn't need much basis in fact; it could come from private paranoia, as with Eminem and Kanye West; still, at some level, it had to be genuine. That, in large part, was why even the best of rappers had a short shelf life. A few triple-platinum albums, a mansion, a Mariah or Beyoncé on your arm, and it was hard to summon up the authentic primal roar.

Che didn't have the platinum album or the mansion, let alone a Maroncé, and he didn't seem to have much righteous rancor either. Affordable Comforts wasn't merely the name of his business. He lived in them.

He told me once that, when he wrote his best songs, he'd been driven by feelings of resentment and confusion, feelings he must write out, or implode. The same feelings had powered "The Prophet" and "Bayuka," less than a year ago. By contrast, the man who slouched around the house on Solomon Street—nudging thirty-five, hemmed in by family and responsibilities and debts— seemed ready to settle, ten cents on the dollar.

Not me. The more passive Che became, the more I boiled. Day after day, I sat in the deserted studio, impotent and seething. When I shaved, the erstwhile Triksta in the mirror was whey-faced and borderline loony. I looked as if I were auditioning for King Lear.

Walking to the grocery store one afternoon, I was jostled by a black teenager and whirled, ready to jump in his face. The teen took one look at me and burst out laughing. This, though hum-bling, was dumb luck. I needed to get a grip on myself—*wind my neck down,* in the Ulster phrase—or I was liable to make a pre-mature exit.

Instead of waiting around for Che, I went back to walking the city. Although the projects were being dismantled, people were still living amid the wreckage and the streets were as murderous as ever. Every night brought a fresh rash of shootings; every day, more buryings. I asked a black cop in a coffee shop how things were going. "Business as usual," he said. I thought not. In the past, whatever the body count, the streets had always been vivid. Now there was blankness, a drop-down weariness more mortal than any grief.

Futility. Nothing was going to change here. Life would never be better. Year after year, generation after generation, the cycle of slaughter would go on, the poverty, the hopelessness, and the end-less, mindless waste. New Orleans, sacrificed to the tourist trade, was dying for real. And hardly anyone seemed to care.

*　　*　　*

Seventh Ward Snoop cared.

He and his partner Shorty Brown Hustle—B—were old com-
padres of Che's who came from the area around Hunter's Field,
the ancient stomping grounds of the Yellow Pocahontas, among
the most celebrated of Mardi Gras Indian tribes. When they'd
started rapping in high school, they named themselves The Power
Rangers. These days, in their mid-twenties, they were simply Da
Rangaz.

Along with their producer, the legendary DJ Chicken, none of
them came much past my armpits, yet their spirit was monumen-
tal. From a distance, they looked like rowdy schoolkids and
appearances didn't lie. By their own admission, they weren't the
slickest of rappers, but they were born performers, guaranteed to
turn out any club or hall that booked them. Unfortunately, they
didn't know when to cease and desist, so they never had a spare
dollar between them. "We got nothing. Even my name belongs to
someone else," said Snoop. Their cell phones were always getting
cut off, they had to work three jobs each just to keep afloat, they
hustled, they cut corners, they drove everyone who dealt with
them nuts. They were New Orleans.

Che had once been their manager. They'd had a bounce song,
"Every Day of My Life," that was a hit from Baton Rouge to Mon-
roe, and had spent a long summer touring Louisiana in a beat-up
van, driving through the night with the radio on. To Snoop, it was
still the highlight of his career: "Stardom could never match that
struggle. The grind is what defines your character, that's where
the magic is," he said. "The vibe we created was a spiritual bond
that can never be broken. Puff Daddy, he can't have it, Jay-Z
neither. Those people are ruled by worldly craving, but real success isn't what you crave. It's what you already have."

No rapper I knew was deeper steeped in street lore than Snoop
or had a sharper view of what was really happening to this town.
Eloquence was his stock in trade. You could throw any word in

the air, and he'd riff for ten minutes without catching breath. Born to freestyle, that was Snoop. At first look—a squat, light-skinned man with bugged-out eyes and jeans sagging below his knees— he was a cartoon of the gutta gangsta. That was camouflage. In reality, both his raising and his own life were staunch moralists. His father was a house painter, his mother a special ed teacher, and Snoop himself had degrees in sociology and criminal justice. When he wasn't busy rapping, he worked as a juvenile parole officer.

His view of New Orleans politics was ground-level, and sulfurous. "We're a black city, and black leaders keep pounding their people every day. Why? Because they feel threatened. They think, 'I can't show that brother how to rise, he might take my spot.' So they crush 'em. They've got their nice houses and nice suits, and all these white folks telling them, 'I like you. You're not like them, those other animals. I can work with you, but those others, they ain't shit.' And the black businessman lets them say it. He doesn't tell them, 'What you mean, *animals*? Those are my brothers down there. They ain't shit, they just misguided.'"

Ray Nagin, the new mayor, was a case in point. One of his campaign promises was that he'd stamp out corruption. Sure enough, soon after his election, he had nailed a grab bag of city employees for illegal sales of brake-tags and paraded them in handcuffs for the TV cameras. "Brake-tags," said Snoop with epic disgust. "Those are poor people sold those tags. The city isn't paying them shit, I know that for a fact, so they try to make a little bit on the side. And the powers that be, they serves 'em up as entertainment. Send out the message loud and clear: 'If you want to be stealing in this town, you better think in millions. Steal you a million, two million, you can sit down with us to dinner. Steal a lousy few hundred bucks, we'll nail your ass to the jailhouse door.'"

Many of the youths he dealt with as a probation officer got even rawer deals. "*No corruption, no crime,* that's the ticket the city's running on, trying to show big business it's safe to come here. So how they do, they'll catch a kid with a nickel bag, slam him in the system. Then he has a record. All he can do the rest of his life is menial work. One nickle bag, and they got 'em a virtual slave."

What to do? It was easy to pound the soapbox, not so simple to come up with concrete solutions. New Orleans had been poisoned since its inception, dirty dealing its second nature. What made Snoop believe it could ever clean up its act? "That's on us. All of us rappers," he said. Not that he thought rap alone could cure all the city's ills; he wasn't starry-eyed. Still, it could be a teacher. If they had the will, rappers could supply the guidance kids no longer received in most classrooms. Instead, they glorified murder. He'd been at a second line on Martin Luther King, and this kid had had his brains blown out all over the sidewalk. His mother was called to the scene. She saw her son dead, lying in his blood. And some of the rappers that were there, they saw it all, yet they still got on a record and talked about busting heads. "That's unacceptable. They're selling their souls behind a dollar. Every rapper in New Orleans keeps saying the same shit, *I'ma shoot ya, I'ma kill ya, I'ma blow out ya brains,* that's the only way they can sell down here. We've been desensitized so far, we can't see we're doing the white man's dirty work. Black people are losing. We're dying out here, and who gives a fuck? Get a deal, get the gold. Make a million-dollar video for BET and tell the world how they shot all these niggas, left their mamas crying. Then they put their name on a foundation, the Big Ass Fund, and throw a little spare change to the ghetto. And meanwhile they're wearing a forty-thousand-dollar bracelet. How can they live with themselves? Don't they know what they are? *106 & Park,* that's a minstrel show. All these rappers, they're nothing but Sambos." He took a ragged breath; his eyes were so wide and engorged, they looked ready to pop their sockets. "Sambos," he said again. "Me too."

*   *   *

December dragged on, and still nothing usable came out of the studio. We were no longer even talking the same musical language. I had brought two hundred CDs south with me, a treasure trove of samples. They came in all styles, from seventies Cambodian pop to John Adams, from Cheb Khaled to Thelonious Monk. Neither Will nor Che showed any interest in exploring them. Sometimes I'd persuade one or the other to listen to a few tracks, and the response was dutiful at best. I felt I was force-feeding them medicine.

At Christmas, I went home to New York for ten days. Maybe, with me gone, Che would feel freed. He could live in the studio if he wanted; Will had already moved in, and, when we talked on the phone, he sounded drunk and happy. He and Che were in the studio all night every night, he said. They'd had some knock-down, drag-out arguments, and everything was better now. The energy was back; they'd made a killer new song. "You won't believe it when you hear it," said Will, and he was right: when I heard it, I didn't believe it. Instead of a cosmic combustion, there was a little sex song on a lazy beat, not terrible, not much of anything. Che's verses sounded as though they'd been read off cue cards. Had I not known better, I would have said he couldn't rap.

How could this be? If I was certain of one thing, it was that Che possessed great gifts. He had written songs and rapped verses that could hold their own in any company. So why wasn't he able to deliver now? Was it me? Too much pressure? Will's beats? Or was it something else?

We sat and talked. I had come to hate these meetings, and Che must have dreaded them too, though he made no complaint. He accepted that he was far off his own standards. He had prayed on it, he said, and still inspiration didn't come. All he could do was fall back on the trusty standbys. The studio wasn't set up right. He needed stronger beats, a fatter sound. We really ought to go to Birmingham.

Watching him—disconsolate, conflicted, struggling for answers—I thought I'd seen the same look someplace before, and after a while I remembered where: Olivier's Hamlet. So this was what we'd come to: Lear and Hamlet with a Pro Tools.

There seemed no point in hammering. I knew some things myself about losing the compass, having once spent three years writing and rewriting a single page. By those standards, Che was barely behind schedule; best let him go free. So we moved the studio out of Solomon Street. His partner Kelwynn's house in the East possessed a box-like brick annex, ten feet square, behind a steel-plated door, where Che could work at his own pace, answering to no one. As for going to Birmingham, I-10 East ran almost by Kelwynn's door; he could hit it any day he chose. From here on, I would back off. Back off? One more step and I'd be neck-deep in Lake Pontchartrain.

Saddi Khali, an old acquaintance of Will's, was a rapper/poet/performance artist who came into the mix as a potential collaborator and became something akin to my spirit guide. On bleak afternoons when nothing else was shaking, we'd meet and talk. And in Saddi's story, and the conflict between his divided selves, I came to hear a narrative for all of black New Orleans; all rap.

He looked Creole, the color of saffron, but his background was as complex as his soul, and that was complex indeed. At thirty, lean and coiled, there was a wild light in his eyes, quick to both anger and joy. His laugh was a high-pitched cackle; his body, never still, danced and whiplashed as we talked. There was, I felt, something feral in him: a consuming hunger, barely held at bay.

Saddi's people came from the Seventh Ward, though his mother's parents had moved to New York in the 1960s. "My mother had the benefit of growing up around people who'd been informed by Malcolm X. She was immersed in Africanness; what had been lost in the Middle Passage." That was how she'd met Saddi's father, a Muslim and a jazzman, an older man who had other women, but she was smitten anyway and gave birth to Saddi—Saddi Sangour Ibn Abou Khali. *Saddi*, in Arabic, means *faithful man; Sangour* means *gift from God.*

When the father fell prey to drugs and turned violent, Saddi's mother left him and came back to New Orleans. Many politicized blacks moved south in the seventies; the FBI was less organized down there. Saddi was raised by a loose-knit community that shared housing and parenting, outside the American system. Most of his childhood was spent traveling around the country, living with people he didn't know. It was a world of black independent schools, New Africa scout troops, ex–Black Panthers. From the ages of two to six, Saddi was made to wear long blond dreadlocks to the small of his back. Outsiders called him Goldilocks and he wished his name was Bobby, Jr. It sounded a cool, all-American name.

He came from a family of seekers. One cousin was a Yoruba priest, his stepfather was a Rasta, and his mother became a priestess in an Ancient Egyptian faith. Saddi, home-schooled, was taught discipline, self-defense, survivalism. He marched in uniform, learned how to shoot a gun, and had it drummed into him that he must never fail. "I was raised as a shining black prince, with an unyielding love for black people and a hunger to conquer oppression. Every day I was told I must rise to embrace our greatness."

This worked fine so long as he stayed in the community. When it came time to go to public school, he felt like an alien. Nothing had prepared him for a culture of TV shows and sports heroes, let alone the labyrinth of drivers' licenses and banks and credit ratings that would await him as an adult. "I came too late. Malcolm was dead and the rest of the charismatic black leaders were on the run. I was born as the dream was shattering but raised as though it was still alive and would return. Everything I was taught was for a world that doesn't exist."

Hip-hop was his hiding place. It took him into the streets, for which he wasn't equipped. "Most of my life, I'd been brainwashed into the African way. I didn't know how to deal with regular black people, wasn't taught to see the me in them. Ghetto shit was overwhelming to me." Perhaps that was why he found it so alluring. He saw the dope dealer and the status he enjoyed, higher than any fallen leader, and how the dealer didn't distance himself. No matter how rich he became, he was still involved with his people, buying old ladies groceries, coaching football teams in the park. "They weren't bad guys, they were stars. Every black male of my father's generation took a left turn when *Superfly* came out. In my generation, it was *Scarface*. And I was deeply affected by that. I didn't have the fearlessness of jail or the insensitivity to consequences to deal dope myself, but I wanted to live lavishly, not glamorize poverty. I started recognizing the duality—Africa inside me, the ghetto outside—and wrestle with the belief that there was bad shit you had to do to get good shit. My mother would be so disappointed to know I thought like that, but I had to say, *Fuck it, I pay my own rent.*"

So many contradictions; he felt himself ripped apart. And there were other causes of conflict, childhood scars that wouldn't heal. In one of his poems, "Me on Happy Endings," he wrote:

> *12yr old cousin lucky*
> *forces his penis*
> *into 4yr old saddi's mouth*
> *& urinates*
> *saddi dies*
> *his parents don't know.*
> *for the next 6 months*

saddi endures various forms
of abuse & torture
at the hands of cousin lucky
& his death goes unnoticed.
it is not the end . . .

Out of torment he created an alter ego, Dirty Red, who was everything that Saddi had been schooled to despise. "Red is where my vices live. Women, vodka cranberry, the guns in my house and the porn on my computer, my anger at being molested. The anger doesn't go away. It's in the wrath that ensues whenever I'm violated in any way. I feel remolested. Saddi can't cope with it, but Dirty Red can."

He saw himself as Janus-faced: "I'm a Pisces, split down the middle. There's a poetry fish and a thug fish, one swimming upstream, one down, trying to find balance. Red doesn't exist without pain. I'd like to kill him off, but there is nothing that celebrates the wholly righteous man in this place and time. That shit don't pay my mortgage."

Saddi wrote poems, and Dirty Red rapped, and the two of them in partnership were struggling businessmen. Saddi wrote,

I have things in me
that will hurt you
sharp objects
that cut and splay flesh.
many leave wounded
heads dangling
limbs held by skin.
i live in fear
of the pain
i cause & keep
dangerous things

hidden like shards of glass
in sand.

But Red, sitting on the stoop, broke and wasted, watching the slim fine women and the big fine women walk by in the soft light of evening, said:

> *Ladies with nice curves*
> *ain't tryin' to hear nuthin'*
> *'bout niggaz who strugglin'*
> *or tryin' to be their husband.*

"If it ain't gangsta, I can't even spit it outta my mouth," Che said. He said a lot of stuff like that these days; it seemed to bolster his nerve. Since moving the studio to the East, he'd surrounded himself with old friends and running pardners, and their imprint was omnipresent. His new songs dealt with sex addiction and dope runs. "The Prophet" was consigned to the back burner.

The studio was a bunker, windowless and unventilated. After a few minutes, the lack of oxygen left me dizzy and I had to escape into the backyard. But Che stuck it out for hours on end, hunkered over the Pro Tools, seemingly oblivious to everything beyond the tracks he kept playing and replaying, times without number.

Kelwynn's house was a brick ranch-style, surrounded by hundreds of other brick ranch-styles. Out here, nothing said New Orleans; we could have been in any suburb in America. No rot, no beauty, no scent of tea olive or jasmine, just row after row of tract homes, each with its own gas-guzzler and wide-screened TV. Twenty years ago, the East had been a promised land. For those trapped in the battle zones, it meant escape. *Be good,* the city told them. *Have patience, play nice, and some day, who knows, we might let you have a driveway, a patch of front lawn, maybe your own tree.* "It was beautiful then. You could take a walk after dark," Will Nelson told me once, with something close to awe. Now, he said, it was gone to hell. As the projects were razed and old neighborhoods gentrified, an endless succession of rehousing initiatives—city, state, federal—had been trumped by the traditional New Orleans mix of corruption and incompetence. Along with working families, the East was flooded with dope dealers and gangbangers. Night-time strolling was no longer advised.

Years before, I'd been shown a portfolio of architect's drawings for a new sub-development off Bullard Avenue. Many of the dwellings featured dogs—fluffy, petable pooches. The slavering cur in the yard across from the studio, frantically trying to tunnel to freedom under a chain-link fence, was not one of those. It never got out and never stopped trying. The same sense of bare containment, liable to break at any moment, pervaded the East as a whole.

Now that Che was in charge, some of his former assurance returned. Instead of brooding on household problems and chasing behind a dollar, he started talking about making a classic album again. Changing the world was back in style.

My own involvement was much reduced. When Che called me to let me hear something new he was working on, he gave every appearance of caring what I thought. Listened gravely to all criticisms and suggestions. And then ignored them. If an album was ever completed, what would be my credit? Executive producer? Mentor? *Money by Triksta* was closer to the mark.

A completed album, meanwhile, still seemed as remote as ever. Che, having shucked me off his back, was now in flight from Will. According to Will, they kept setting up sessions and Che kept vanishing. When Will arrived at the studio, the steel door would be locked. Since he had no key and nobody offered to give him one, he'd sit in his car for hours, talking to females on his cell phone, and finally drive home, nothing accomplished. "You know what this is?" he said to me. "This is fucked up."

All three of us were getting ragged and ugly. Though Will always sustained a gentlemanly façade, at least in my presence, I knew he had lost faith in me. Once he'd been in the habit of quoting his mother, who told him I was sent to him for a reason. Nothing along those lines was mentioned anymore. Instead, I became more and more conscious of pent-up resentment. He never confronted me, yet the tension was palpable. False father, I had failed him. Sometimes, when he thought I wasn't paying attention, I'd catch him staring at me. It was not a look of love.

In essence, Che was making his album on his own. His knowledge of Pro Tools was still rudimentary, if that, but he pressed doggedly ahead. Every time I passed through he was head-down over the computer, playing back some track, over and over, ten times, twenty, as if it contained a buried encryption that, once deciphered, would make him master of the rap universe. Over time, the rear view of his big shoulders, slumped with exhaustion, became my abiding image of him.

The longer I knew him, the more layers I found and the less I could pass blanket judgments. Away from the studio, he could be warm and easy company. When Michaela was in town, he talked to her for hours about his children, his love of *The Sopranos,* and a hundred other commonplace matters. Even she, however, couldn't predict his moods. Every day he seemed to point in a different direction. Now I'd distanced myself, he called constantly. One minute he sounded euphoric, full of ideas; the next, he was lost again. When asked, he always claimed that he was fine, no problem, though his body language told another story. In dark moods, his face collapsed like a fallen soufflé.

I had rarely wished more devoutly to help any man, rarely felt so useless. And time was running short. Before we'd set to work in the fall, I had set an unbreakable deadline of March first. On that day, no matter what, I was going to blow the whistle, pack up the studio and head back north, in triumph or defeat. If the schedule was arbitrary, I also felt it was imperative. Without it, at the rate things were going, we could be here in a year, two years, and still have nothing to show. The winter chill had gone; Solomon Street was in flower. Sunlight filtered through the Thrift City curtains, and Will tried to reassure me. "I'm not worried," he kept saying. He and Che had finally hooked up, and they had some new tracks I should hear.

These tracks proved surprisingly soft and fuzzy, reflecting their shared love of old-school, marshmallow-centered R&B. Flutes were much in evidence, and drifty little keyboard figures. To someone who loves hard beats, it sounded like rap lite.

One song, "I-10 West," dealt with the drug runs to Houston that were a time-honored rite of passage for New Orleans youth. Generations, cash hungry, had made the same trek; the interstate was a pilgrim road. "Pick up your guns, strap on your vest," the hook began, even though Che, in a belated nod to responsibility, ended the song with a long spiel about drugs not being the only path to riches and how becoming a doctor was even better.

I listened with bemusement. *Pick up your guns?* Che was about as lethal as I was. His father's home, which he shared, was in a gated community, with a level of security that made my place on Solomon Street look like a squat. As desperadoes go, he was strictly fasten-the-seatbelt, check-the-rearview-mirror. Yet here he came rapping, in all seriousness, like Soulja Slim resurrected. And his support group was all for it. They, too, by New Orleans standards, were middle-class. They sold advertising, drove taxis, or ran their own businesses. Even Tom Beez, who'd walked the wild side in his time, had a construction firm. Nor were they youngsters; the average age was over thirty. These were solid citizens, the present and future of the city, yet they were hooked on an imagined past. Much as aging rock fans at a Bruce Springsteen or Rolling Stones concert will hold up cigarette lighters and sway together in the dark, remembering glory days that never were, so the men shoehorned into this bunker listening to "I-10 West" loved to bullshit about a mythical time when they ran the streets and no job was waiting to take its revenge in the morning, and the cash in their pockets wasn't spoken for by bills, and every next female they met might be the one to give them all that freak shit they'd seen in porn videos, and they'd felt invincible.

Here, more real than the gold-tooth ballers and dime pieces on BET, was the profile of hip-hop now: a man or woman approaching middle age, with a job, a house, a mortgage. They had listened to rap from infancy, "Rapper's Delight" was likely the first record they had loved, and the music was meshed so deeply into their lives that they couldn't picture an existence without it. No longer just the noise from the streets, it was in the weave of day-to-day, of car rides and family gatherings, the soundtrack of paying the bills, no less than clubs or block parties. "Hip-hop," as Che said, "is who we are."

If he had the nerve to tackle these truths, he might not draw the headlines of 50 Cent and Eminem or end up Croesus-rich, but I thought he could do quite nicely, thank you. Once, in Solomon Street, I sicced Saddi on him, and Saddi berated him for rapping stuff that wasn't in his own experience. "Why don't you write about paying the mortgage or selling cars?" he demanded. Che just stared at him, tortoise-like, his head sunk so deep into his chest that his neck all but vanished. "I feel you," he said. Then he wrote a rap about sex addiction. "The Reluctant Pimp," he called it.

The culture of braggadocio was so ingrained, nothing could shift it. That had been hip-hop's birth cry—"I AM, muthafucka!"— and rap had never moved on. Even for those who lived worlds away from the combat zone and had never known a day's hardship, the blueprint was set in stone. Or was it? Somebody else would have to find out; I was done. Evaluating Che's new tracks, I heard nothing I could identify with. All the other records I'd been involved with, from Choppa on, had possessed some common thread. Though I couldn't claim to have created any single song, my mark was on each of them. When I combined them on a CD— *Da Triksta Muthalode*?—the sum of the whole expressed me. Parts of me, at any rate. That wasn't true of "I-10 West" or "The Reluctant Pimp," and even less of "So Fly," the easy-listening track that Che and Will were working on now, as Mardi Gras passed and February wore down, and deadline day was almost at hand.

With every day, I felt myself sinking deeper in swamp. Four months had passed without a single completed track. I still believed in Che, in some ways more than ever, though I no longer believed I was his luck. He must make do for himself.

I had failed at every possible level, creative, personal, commercial. My virus was running riot; I was a total wreck. Worse, I was starting to like it. Every night I told myself to stop wasting time and get back to my other life. Then morning came and the phone started ringing. Saddi came around, or Snoop, or some new rapper I'd never met. I took a ride to the bootlegger and bought the new G-Unit album; I dropped by Tee's barbershop; I checked out Bass Heavy's studio. In the back room where the Pro Tools used to be, I listened to Devin the Dude glorify slacker life, while the spring sunlight slanted through the dirt-caked blinds, casting stripes on the rutted floorboards. This, I felt, was my existence now; wasting time was all there was. New Orleans was sucking me under. When I wandered the city, loving and hating it, I hardly saw the violence and misery anymore, and couldn't see the beauty at all. I was conscious only of the smells, and a vast aimlessness.

What had become of my fear? Gone, along with passion and belief. At some point, unknowing, I'd crossed a line. I could feel it by the way Da Rangaz behaved around me. They no longer bothered to put on a show, just shambled in my door and started talking; I'd become furniture. Sometimes they called me their nigga, but that wasn't it. I wasn't looking to be black. Wasn't looking to be anything. For the first time I could recall, I had no goal. I hadn't a clue what I was doing here. Drowning; I knew that much. And I couldn't summon the will to strike out for shore.

It was Shorty Brown Hustle who tossed me a life raft. He was a squirt, a shave-skulled runt with a devilish wit and a mouth that never stopped flapping. No one could run the dozens like B; no one else could have said the things he did without getting killed. He walked up to cripples and mongols and chemo patients, threw their infirmities in their faces, and somehow they took it from him, embraced it even, for there was greatness in his heart, they knew it on sight. He never bragged on himself, yet according to Snoop, who'd known him all their lives, he shared everything he possessed. His two-room apartment was open to all. People came to him in trouble, looking for a night's shelter, and stayed for months, sleeping in his bed while he bunked on the sofa. Half of the rappers in New Orleans had leaned on him at some time, Soulja Slim included, and few gave anything back. That was not the point. Even when they stole from him, B kept on giving. He couldn't seem to help himself.

I had the sense, the first time we met, that he took one look and saw me, all of me, without disguises. He knew me. And I, in turn, knew something of him. There was an instinctive, nerve-end connection between us I'd felt with few other humans. And one night, leaving the house, he said casually, across his shoulder, "All we've got is skin and our souls."

Michaela ended it. If not for her, I might still be by Kelwynn's, squatting outside the bunker, watching the mutt across the yard tunneling to freedom. There would always be one more track to try, another rapper to be heard. K-Gates, for example. He had just turned twenty, and his skills were ungodly. He'd made a couple of mix tapes, one pitting him against 50 Cent, and every line oozed authority. Even Che agreed. We set up a meeting, with a view to putting him on Che's album, and Gates handled himself regally. Presence, hunger, the mix of arrogance and insecurity that all great rappers must possess—he was the total package.

One more shot; just one. What was left to lose? Michaela looked at me levelly, not a word, and went through to the next room and started packing.

The night we broke up the studio was unseasonably cold and dank. Che sat over the computer, burning his tracks onto CD. He was going to take them up to Birmingham, he said, and start over. I couldn't meet his eye.

Will was sitting across the street in his car, talking to a female on his cell. He and Che were barely on speaking terms. Until the final week, Will had convinced himself that all would come good. "I'm not worried yet," he kept repeating, though we were still fourteen tracks shy of an album and I had just rejected "So Fly." It was only on the final day that he admitted defeat. Then he blamed Che bitterly. His life's dream was smashed; Che had failed him. And this was certainly true. But Will had also failed Che, and I had failed them both. Four months, and nothing to show. It boggled the mind.

When Will got off the phone at last, we dismantled the equipment, put it back into its cases, and loaded them in the car. We stood in the street and embraced awkwardly. Che looked stricken; his face had a gray undertint. It felt as though there'd been a death in the family, and I started to weaken. Michaela knew better. She touched my arm, and I climbed into the car, and we drove off. It was finished.

REMIX

Finished. And then it wasn't. A few weeks after I left town, Che at last went to Birmingham and started recording with James Belville and Big Bird. A few more weeks, and we met up in London, courtesy of Slice, a P.R. company that worked with Southern Comfort liquor, which originated in New Orleans. As an indirect result of the article I'd written for *The Guardian Weekend*, Che, Kiane, Da Rangaz, and DJ Chicken had been flown over to England to perform at a music-industry party. Though only Kiane had a passport, and there was a last-minute scramble before they all made the plane, they were waiting at their hotel in Southwark when I arrived from New York.

Ironically, I'd never heard any of them on stage. So many shows in New Orleans had ended in shootings that live performances were almost extinct in the city, and rappers had to go on the road to be heard. In order to see Snoop and Shorty Brown Hustle strut and clamber over the speakers while Chicken worked the wheels of steel, I must travel to the verdant grasslands of Hackney.

The Southern Comfort show was a success, though New Orleans heat was not a natural fit for studied London cool. Not many in the crowd were willing to be caught sweating, though they shuffled their feet and nodded, approximating life.

Che seemed, if not a changed man, emended. He'd lost weight and looked years younger, that was part of it, but the greater shift was in his presence. There was a calm about him, as if he knew where he was going. Che himself said he felt recharged. The night the studio was broken up, he'd felt his insides shrivel. Right up to the last minute, he thought there'd be a reprieve. It was only when he walked indoors and saw the bunker stripped bare that the reality hit. He'd had what he always wanted, and let it slip. He never wanted that feeling again.

Sitting in a sterile hotel lobby with New Age muzak piped in, Che looked me hard in the eye, just as he'd done when we first met and not too often since, and I believed him. We had traveled a long road; all that mileage couldn't be for nothing. *What doesn't kill you makes you crunk.* That's what they said in the Seventh Ward. Or, if they didn't, they should.

When the All-Star Revue returned to America, I started writing this book and Che got down to some serious rapping. He went back to "She Wants Some," and this time he nailed it. When he sent me the CD, I heard a potential hit and shipped the studio back to Kelwynn's, half-expecting that having it again, permanently at his disposal, would return him to paralysis. I was wrong. New songs kept accruing, more and more CDs kept showing up in my mail. And Che was not the only one galvanized. Da Rangaz used the studio to start recording an entire album, and Tom Beez seemed almost to live there. Then K-Gates started calling me, pushing his new mix tape. Kiane, who had lost patience with New Orleans and moved to Atlanta, was working on new material; DJ Chicken had made a rock 'n' bounce tape; Jahbo won a Crescent City Idol contest and a studio date with Mannie Fresh of Cash Money. Even Junie B got back in touch. She said she'd been offered a deal at Avatar, a limb of Atlantic records, and she wanted me to become her manager. I knew I'd be lousy at the job and had to turn her down, but merely to be asked puffed me up like a pouter pigeon.

Da Rangaz' album, *Drunk-Ass Muzik,* was another plus. They had recorded it in the dog days of summer, banged up inside Kelwynn's bunker, 110 degrees and no air. Penniless, out of work, sometimes short of food, with one car and one phone between them, they'd slept many nights on the studio floor but had stuck it out regardless, and the results were mighty. Hearing them run amok over DJ Chicken's drum-heavy tracks, everything that I'd felt five years ago at the Money Wasters parade, the first time I experienced bounce up close, came surging back at me. The grime and heat and pure mad lust for being alive, *Drunk-Ass Muzik* caught it all.

This being New Orleans, nothing came quickly or simply. For every new track that showed up, half a dozen went missing in action. Still, good things were astir. They might translate into commercial success, or not. Either way, I had no more cash to put up and was reduced to cheerleading. The music, not the game, was all that remained.

In the months since I left Solomon Street, my years in the rap game had taken on a new perspective. I no longer thought of failures or damage. Instead, I saw a great gift. The names alone— Jubilee, Katey Red, Choppa, Bigg Ramp, Big Man, Big D, Big Slack, King George, Lil Mel, Lil Tee, Supa Dave, Playa Will, DJ Duck, DJ Chicken, DJ Money Fresh, DJ Ron, Sinista, Wydell, White Dave, Don Juan, Fess, Soulja Slim, 5th Ward Weebie, Mobo Joe, Hot Boy Ronald, Josephine Johnny, P-Town Moe, Bass Heavy, Earl and Poochie Mackie, Henry the Man, Junie B, Lisa Amos, Tek-9 and Lil' Ya, Money, B-Red, Baby Boy, Stevee, Che Muse, Tom Beez, Kiane, Seventh Ward Snoop, Shorty Brown Hustle, K-Gates, Saddi Khali—seemed an honor roll. I'd never known greater richness.

The riches, I saw at last, had never been where I'd looked for them. Nothing I thought I was likely to achieve panned out. Recharge my fires? I was brought to my knees. A challenge? I fell at every hurdle. Create rap classics? Forget it. I had tried to shape a narrative—*The Triksta's Tale*—and instead it shaped me. Finally, whatever I had or hadn't accomplished in terms of deals or hits or credits was irrelevant. Only when I accepted this did I start to get my reward.

During those last drowning weeks at Solomon Street, I had finally ceased to plot and maneuver. For once in my life, I ceded control. And this had proved my salvation. I was no longer Triksta or Mort Ziploc, just Nik, caught up in rap. Not one of the boyz, of course; I could never be that. Still, a soldier in my own style.

And what of the deeper journey, begun in the Iberville? It is too soon and I'm still standing too close to offer gift-wrapped conclusions. I can't swear that, swarmed again, I would react differently; on the whole, I doubt it. Racial memory and fear aren't such cosmetic trifles that a few quick seasons in the trenches are likely to have wiped out all trace of them. What I have learned is not to go to the Iberville unasked in the first place, not as small a thing as it may sound. The last five years, if nothing else, have cured my taste for quixotic gestures. When viral (or other) lunacies strike these days, I shut myself in a room and rage at walls. There is no *they* to confront. The thugs are in me.

As I write this, my flight is booked again. Soon I'll be back in New Orleans, recording in Bass Heavy's new studio on the West Bank. But that's not what I'm going for, not really. What I crave is the moment when Che and Da Rangaz bring a new track to wherever I'm staying and we go outside and listen on the car speakers. When the bass kicks in, the bodywork starts to vibrate and half a dozen heads bob as one, and the rappers take turns to spit verses, each line a verbal snapshot of this city that has me by the balls and will until I die. In that moment, nothing else exists. All we've got is skin and our souls.